2nd International Workshop on Computational Approaches to Historical Language Change (LChange'21)

Held online due to COVID-19

Bangkok, Thailand
6 August 2021

ISBN: 978-1-7138-3379-6

LChange'21

The 2nd International Workshop on Computational Approaches to Historical Language Change 2021

Proceedings of the Workshop

August 6, 2021
Bangkok, Thailand (online)

IGUANODON AI
Your Brussels-Based Language Technology and Data Science Company

Message from Organizers

Welcome to the 2nd International Workshop on Computational Approaches to Historical Language Change (LChange'21) co-located with ACL-IJCNLP 2021 on August 6, 2021 and held virtually. Following the success of the first workshop organized at ACL 2019, we are pleased to present the proceedings of the second installment of this workshop series.

The sociocultural and technological development in the world is closely connected to our language as a means to facilitate efficient communication. As a consequence, human language changes over time. Traces of these changes are apparent in our texts and important to anyone who either directly studies changing phenomena, or who uses diachronic texts as a basis for their studies. This workshop explores the phenomena of language change found in written text, on the topics of computational methodologies, theories and digital text resources for exploring the time-varying nature of human language. Its aim is three-fold. First, we want to provide an outlet for pioneering researchers who work on computational methods, evaluation, and large-scale modelling of language change to disseminate cutting-edge research on topics concerning language change. We intended this workshop as a platform for sharing state-of-the-art research progress in this fundamental domain of natural language research. Second, we want to bring together domain experts across disciplines including but not restricted to linguistics, natural language processing, computer science, cognitive psychology, history and digital humanities. Third, the detection and modelling of language change using diachronic text and text mining raise fundamental theoretical and methodological challenges for future research in this area. We hope to engage corpus and computational linguists, (big-) data scientists, as well as humanities and social science scholars to address these open issues.

In response to the call we received 16 submissions.[1] Each of them was carefully evaluated by three members of the Program Committee, whom we believed to be most appropriate for each paper. Based on the reviewers' feedback we accepted 9 full and short papers as oral presentations or as poster papers. We had two distinguished keynote presentations: the first by Maria Koptjevskaja-Tamm (Stockholm University) and Tatiana Nikitina (LLACAN – "Languages and cultures of Africa", CNRS) who presented a talk titled "Linguistic diversity as a testing ground for the study of semantic change", and the second by Alexander Koplenig (Leibniz-Institute for the German Language in Mannheim) with the talk "Two challenges we face when analyzing diachronic corpora". Finally, we have invited 6 findings papers from ACL2021 to be presented either orally or as posters, which are not included in the workshop proceedings.

We hope that you will find the workshop papers insightful and inspiring. We would like to thank the keynote speakers for their stimulating talks, the authors of all papers for their interesting contributions and the members of the Program Committee for their insightful reviews. Our special thanks go to the emergency reviewers who stepped in to provide their expertise. We also express our gratitude to the ACL 2021 workshop chairs for their kind assistance during the organisation process, and for arranging the logistics and infrastructure allowing us to hold LChange'21 online. Finally, our thanks go towards our silver sponsor iguanodon.ai.

Nina Tahmasebi, workshop chair, University of Gothenburg (Sweden)
Adam Jatowt, University of Innsbruck (Austria)
Yang Xu, University of Toronto (Canada)
Simon Hengchen, University of Gothenburg (Sweden)
Syrielle Montariol, INRIA Paris (France)
Haim Dubossarsky, University of Cambridge (United Kingdom)
LChange'21 Workshop Chairs

---

[1] The number of submissions is a significant drop from the 2019 workshop, following a trend of lower workshop submissions as a consequence of the Covid pandemic.

Organizing Committee:

Nina Tahmasebi, workshop chair, University of Gothenburg (Sweden)
Adam Jatowt, University of Innsbruck (Austria)
Yang Xu, University of Toronto (Canada)
Simon Hengchen, University of Gothenburg (Sweden)
Syrielle Montariol, INRIA Paris (France)
Haim Dubossarsky, University of Cambridge (United Kingdom)

Program Committee:

Ehsaneddin Asgari, University of California, Berkeley (United States)
Zhenisbek Assylbekov, Nazarbayev University (Kazakhstan)
Pierpaolo Basile, Department of Computer Science, University of Bari Aldo Moro (Italy)
Christin Beck, University of Konstanz (Germany)
Barend Beekhuizen, University of Toronto (Canada)
Klaus Berberich, Saarbruecken University of Applied Sciences (Germany)
Chris Biemann, University of Hamburg (Germany)
Damián Blasi, Harvard University and Max Planck Institute for the Science of Human History (United States)
Annalina Caputo, Dublin City University, ADAPT Centre, I-Form Centre (Ireland)
Pierluigi Cassotti, University of Bari Aldo Moro (Italy)
Brady Clark, Northwestern University (United States)
Paul Cook, University of New Brunswick (Canada)
Yijun Duan, AIST (Japan)
Michael Färber, Karlsruhe Institute of Technology (Germany)
Lauren Fonteyn, Leiden University (Netherlands)
Karlien Franco, KU Leuven (Belgium)
Mario Giulianelli, University of Amsterdam (Netherlands)
Maurício Gruppi, Rensselaer Polytechnic institute (United States)
Mika Hämäläinen, University of Helsinki (Finland)
Ran Iwamoto, Keio University (Japan)
Vaibhav Jain, Independent Scholar (India)
Abhik Jana, University of Hamburg (Germany)
Tommi Jauhiainen, University of Helsinki (Finland)
Péter Jeszenszky, University of Bern (Switzerland)
Richard Johansson, University of Gothenburg (Sweden)
Jens Kaiser, University of Stuttgart (Germany)
Vani Kanjirangat, IDSIA (Switzerland)
Andres Karjus, University of Tartu (Estonia)
Tom Kenter, Google UK (United Kingdom)
Andrey Kutuzov, University of Oslo (Norway)
Anna Marakasova, TU Wien (Austria)
Matej Martinc, Jozef Stefan Institute (Slovenia)
Barbara McGillivray, The Alan Turing Institute and University of Cambridge (United Kingdom)
Filip Miletic, CLLE, CNRS /University of Toulouse (France)
Animesh Mukherjee, IIT Kharagpur (India)
Kjetil Norvag, NTNU (Norway)
Krzysztof Nowak, Institute of Polish Language (Poland)

Paul Nulty, University College Dublin (Ireland)
Maike Park, Leibniz-Institute for German Language (Germany)
Stefano De Pascale, KU Leuven (Belgium)
Xutan Peng, The University of Sheffield (United Kingdom)
Peter Petré, University of Antwerp (Belgium)
Lidia Pivovarova, University of Helsinki (Finland)
Martin Pömsl, Osnabrück University (Germany)
Pavel Přibáň, University of West Bohemia (Czech Republic)
Taraka Rama, University of North Texas at Denton (United States)
Julia Rodina, National Research University Higher School of Economics (Russia)
Eyal Sagi, Northwestern University (United States)
Tanja Säily, University of Helsinki (Finland)
Dominik Schlechtweg, University of Stuttgart (Germany)
Sandeep Soni, Georgia Institute of Technology (United States)
Andreas Spitz, University of Konstanz (Germany)
Ian Stewart, University of Michigan (United States)
Suzanne Stevenson, University of Toronto (Canada)
Ludovic Tanguy, CLLE: University of Toulouse and CNRS (France)
Stephen Taylor, University of West Bohemia (Czech Republic)
Rocco Tripodi, Alma Mater Studiorum - University of Bologna (Italy)
Melvin Wevers, DHLAB, KNAW Humanities Cluster (Netherlands)
Ekaterina Vylomova, University of Melbourne (Australia)
Frank D. Zamora-Reina, University of Chile (Chile)
Yihong Zhang, Osaka University (Japan)
Elaine Zosa, University of Helsinki (Finland)

Invited Speakers:

Alexander Koplenig, Leibniz-Institute for the German Language in Mannheim (Germany)
Maria Koptjevskaja-Tamm, Stockholm University (Sweden)
Tatiana Nikitina, LLACAN – "Languages and cultures of Africa", CNRS (France)

Keynote abstracts:

Keynote 1

Speakers: Maria Koptjevskaja-Tamm, Stockholm University (Sweden) and Tatiana Nikitina, LLACAN – "Languages and cultures of Africa", CNRS (France)

Title of talk: **Linguistic diversity as a testing ground for the study of semantic change**

Abstract: There are between 6000 and 8000 languages currently spoken in the world. The majority of those still lack decent descriptions, not to mention any written tradition and sizeable documents to rely on while trying to trace semantic changes they have undergone in the past and understanding the mechanisms behind them. Understandably, but likewise regrettably, most of the theoretical thinking in linguistics and adjacent disciplines has been formed by research on a few very big languages with a long written tradition, and the same has to a large extent been carried over to computational approaches, including work on semantic change. In our talk we will focus on two big issues which we believe deserve more awareness and attention among researchers involved in computational approaches to historical language change:

- A crucial part in any theoretical work consists of formulating hypotheses, generalizations, laws etc. and explaining them, and work on semantic change is, of course, no exception. Linguistic diversity does not imply that any such generalizations are meaningless or premature before these have been studied for all the world's languages. It does imply, though, that such generalizations gain a lot from careful systematic cross-linguistic research that may unveil cross-linguistic regularities behind diversity – which is foundational for linguistic typology. Here we will discuss several cases whereby such research has questioned earlier generalizations on semantic change based on the familiar languages and/or has come up with new hypotheses.

- But given that the majority of the world's languages lack any written tradition and sizeable historical documents, how is it possible to study semantic changes they have undergone in the past? This is indeed a big challenge, but not an insurmountable one. We will discuss several methods which often combine a careful intragenetic comparison (i.e., comparison of closely related languages) and a broader cross-linguistic perspective and some of the results obtained by their application.

Keynote 2

Speaker: Alexander Koplenig, Leibniz-Institute for the German Language in Mannheim (Germany)

Title of talk: **Two challenges we face when analyzing diachronic corpora.**

Abstract: In my keynote, I want to discuss two important challenges for the quantitative analysis of diachronic corpora that I believe deserve more attention:

- The first challenge is the systematic influence of the sample size when it comes to basically all measures in quantitative linguistics (Baayen 2001). By analysing the lexical dynamics of the German weekly news magazine "Der Spiegel" (consisting of approximately 365,000 articles and 237,000,000 words that were published between 1947 and 2017), I show that this influence makes it difficult to quantify lexical dynamics and language change. I will also demonstrate that standard sampling approaches do not solve this problem. I will suggest an approach that is able to break the sample size dependence but presupposes access to the full text data (Koplenig, Wolfer & Müller-Spitzer 2019).

- The second challenge is of methodological nature and relates to the problem of representativeness of diachronic corpora. Labov (1994) famously stated that "historical documents survive by chance, not by design, and the selection that is available is the product of an unpredictable series of historical accidents." By using both Google Books Ngram data (Michel et al. 2010; Koplenig 2015; Pechenick, Danforth & Dodds 2015) and publicly available data from the German National Bibliography, I will try to show that the problem is even more fundamental, because there is good reason to believe that composition of the body of published written works (from which a corresponding corpus is supposed to be sampled from) systematically changes as a function of time. This makes it difficult to disentangle actual language change from environmental changes in the textual habitat (Szmrecsanyi 2016).

Table of Contents

Time-Aware Ancient Chinese Text Translation and Inference
Ernie Chang, Yow-Ting Shiue, Hui-Syuan Yeh and Vera Demberg 1

Three-part diachronic semantic change dataset for Russian
Andrey Kutuzov and Lidia Pivovarova 7

The Corpora They Are a-Changing: a Case Study in Italian Newspapers
Pierpaolo Basile, Annalina Caputo, Tommaso Caselli, Pierluigi Cassotti and Rossella Varvara . . 14

Linguistic change and historical periodization of Old Literary Finnish
Niko Partanen, Khalid Alnajjar, Mika Hämäläinen and Jack Rueter 21

A diachronic evaluation of gender asymmetry in euphemism
Anna Kapron-King and Yang Xu 28

The GLAUx corpus: methodological issues in designing a long-term, diverse, multi-layered corpus of Ancient Greek
Alek Keersmaekers 39

Bhāṣācitra: Visualising the dialect geography of South Asia
Aryaman Arora, Adam Farris, Gopalakrishnan R and Samopriya Basu 51

Modeling the Evolution of Word Senses with Force-Directed Layouts of Co-occurrence Networks
Tim Reke, Robert Schwanhold and Ralf Krestel 58

Tracking Semantic Change in Cognate Sets for English and Romance Languages
Ana Sabina Uban, Alina Maria Cristea, Anca Dinu, Liviu P. Dinu, Simona Georgescu and Laurentiu Zoicas 64

Conference Program

August 6, 2021 [UTC+0]

07:00-07:15 *Introduction*

07:15-08:30 **Session 1**

07:15-07:40 *Time-Aware Ancient Chinese Text Translation and Inference*
Ernie Chang, Yow-Ting Shiue, Hui-Syuan Yeh and Vera Demberg LChange'21

07:40-08:05 *Three-part diachronic semantic change dataset for Russian*
Andrey Kutuzov and Lidia Pivovarova LChange'21

08:05-08:30 *The Corpora They Are a-Changing: a Case Study in Italian Newspapers*
Pierpaolo Basile, Annalina Caputo, Tommaso Caselli, Pierluigi LChange'21
Cassotti and Rossella Varvara

08:30-09:05 *Break*

09:05-09:30 *Linguistic change and historical periodization of Old Literary Finnish*
Niko Partanen, Khalid Alnajjar, Mika Hämäläinen and Jack LChange'21
Rueter

09:30-10:00 *Studying the Evolution of Scientific Topics and their Relationships*
Ana Sabina Uban, Cornelia Caragea and Liviu P. Dinu Findings

10:00-10:30 *When Time Makes Sense: A Historically-Aware Approach to Targeted Sense Disambiguation*
Kaspar Beelen, Federico Nanni, Mariona Coll Arduany, Kasra Findings
Hosseini, Giorgia Tolfo and Barbara McGillivray

10:30-11:30 *Lunch break*

11:30-12:30 **Keynote 1:** *Linguistic diversity as a testing ground for the study of semantic change*
Maria Koptjevskaja-Tamm and Tatiana Nikitina

12:30-14:00 **Online poster session**

A diachronic evaluation of gender asymmetry in euphemism
Anna Kapron-King and Yang Xu LChange'21

The GLAUx corpus: methodological issues in designing a long-term, diverse, multi-layered corpus of Ancient Greek LChange'21
Alek Keersmaekers

Bhāṣācitra: Visualising the dialect geography of South Asia
Aryaman Arora, Adam Farris, Gopalakrishnan R and Samopriya Basu — LChange'21

Modeling the Evolution of Word Senses with Force-Directed Layouts of Co-occurrence Networks
Tim Reke, Robert Schwanhold and Ralf Krestel — LChange'21

Tracking Semantic Change in Cognate Sets for English and Romance Languages
Ana Sabina Uban, Alina Maria Cristea, Anca Dinu, Liviu P. Dinu, Simona Georgescu and Laurentiu Zoicas — LChange'21

Can Cognate Prediction Be Modelled as a Low-Resource Machine Translation Task?
Clementine Fourrier, Rachel Bawden, Benoit Sagot — Findings

Event Extraction from Historical Texts: A New Dataset for Black Rebellions
Viet Dac Lai, Minh Van Nguyen, Heidi Kaufman and Thien Huu Nguyen — Findings

Sequence Models for Computational Etymology of Borrowings
Winston Wu, Kevin Duh, David Yarowsky — Findings

A Formidable Ability: Detecting Adjectival Extremeness with DSMs
Farhan Samir, Barend Beekhuizen and Suzanne Stevenson — Findings

14:00-15:00 **Keynote 2:** *Two challenges we face when analyzing diachronic corpora*
Alexander Koplenig

Time-Aware Ancient Chinese Text Translation and Inference

⋆Ernie Chang[文], ∘Yow-Ting Shiue[文], ⋆Hui-Syuan Yeh, ⋆Vera Demberg
⋆Dept. of Language Science and Technology, Saarland University
∘Dept. of Computer Science, University of Maryland, College Park
{cychang}@coli.uni-saarland.de, ytshiue@cs.umd.edu

Abstract

In this paper, we aim to address the challenges surrounding the translation of ancient Chinese text: (1) The *linguistic gap* due to the difference in eras results in translations that are poor in quality, and (2) most translations are missing the contextual information that is often very crucial to understanding the text. To this end, we improve upon past translation techniques by proposing the following: We reframe the task as a *multi-label prediction task* where the model predicts both the translation and its particular era. We observe that this helps to bridge the linguistic gap as chronological context is also used as auxiliary information. We validate our framework on a parallel corpus annotated with chronology information and show experimentally its efficacy in producing quality translation outputs. We release both the code and the data[1] for future research.

1 Introduction

The Chinese language inherits a lot of phrases from ancient time (Bao-chuan, 2008; Liu, 2019) and is spoken by roughly 1.3 billion native speakers. However, the language's ancient variant (or *ancient Chinese*) is mastered by a few and proved to be a bottleneck in understanding the essence of the Chinese culture. Building a translation system from the ancient Chinese to the modern text thus serves a few important purposes: (I) The ancient Chinese is considered as an essential part of the curriculum in all of the Chinese-speaking regions[2], so an ancient Chinese translation system can be used to bolster the immediate understanding of ancient texts. (II) Further, the translation system can help to settle the

linguistic debate with regard to the era of origin of an independent segment of text. This is especially useful for the identification of a discovered artifacts where carbon dating cannot pinpoint the exact era, but where their linguistic features can formulate a clear-cut dynasty or time period.

However, it is not without challenge in constructing such translation systems. One primary obstacle lies in the extensive timeline where ancient texts can be derived – one segment of ancient text can come from the Pre-Qin (先秦) era, and another coming from the Song dynasty (宋朝), which are roughly about 700 years apart. This gap witnessed a drastic evolution of linguistic properties where the usage of phrases became imbued with different meanings. Besides, different eras often consist of various amounts of available data, and thus the same translation model training will be exposed to data imbalance, which complicates the design of the translation systems and limits their generalizability. On the other hand, past attempts at building such translation systems yield poor performance that renders them practically unusable as-is in the practical settings (Zhang et al., 2018; Liu et al., 2019) – these efforts are still largely limited as parallel data is scarce for some eras.

Recent advances in machine translation and text style transfer/generation utilize semi-supervised techniques to tackle similar challenges by aligning latent representations from different styles for the low resource scenarios (Shen et al., 2017; Hu et al., 2017; Rao and Tetreault, 2018; Prabhumoye et al., 2018; Jin et al., 2019; Chang et al., 2020, 2021c). To this end, we aim to bridge this gap that makes the following contributions:

- We showed that having ancient Chinese text of all eras in a single corpus is not ideal as they are difficult to model jointly as a single distribution, and that the additional *chrono-*

[文]These authors contributed equally.
[1]https://github.com/orina1123/
time-aware-ancient-text-translation
[2]This includes the mainland China, Taiwan, Singapore, Malaysia, etc.

1

Proceedings of the 2nd International Workshop on Computational Approaches to Historical Language Change 2021, pages 1–6
August 6, 2021. ©2021 Association for Computational Linguistics

logical context helps to improve translation of ancient Chinese to modern Chinese sentences.

- For future research in this direction, we release our code and parallel data consisting of annotated *chronological identifiers* which allow to infer the approximate era of the written text in the practical settings.

2   Background

At a fine-grained view, the notion of "ancient Chinese" may not be considered a single language with a static word-meaning mapping. Therefore, we direct our efforts toward three particular eras: Pre-Qin (先秦), Han (汉), and Song (宋) to verify the hypothesis that the chronology of a text directly influences the word meaning and model performance. In particular, *Pre-Qin* and *Han* are closer chronologically, so we expect their model performances to be closer than that between *Pre-Qin* and *Song*, as was shown in other ancient text translation (Park et al., 2020).

One reason for this difference is the use of polysemous single-character words, which are highly ambiguous. Some words begin to lose meanings over time. For example, in ancient Chinese, the word 看('kàn') has many meanings such as "to visit" and "to listen", in addition to the major modern meaning, "to look".

As the language evolved, vocabulary changed and lexical semantic shift took place, creating diachronic semantic gaps that may introduce subtle differences in the understanding of the text. For instance, the earliest known meaning of "看" is "to look into the distance". The meaning of "to look at something closely" emerged during the Han period and eventually became the prominent meaning of this verb in modern Chinese. In sum, the language change across time suggests a modeling approach that is aware of when the text was written.

3   Task Formulation

We assume two nonparallel datasets A and M of sentences in *Ancient Chinese (zh-a)* and *Modern Chinese (zh-m)* respectively. A parallel dataset P that contains the pairs of sentences in both variants of text is also present. The sizes of the three datasets are denoted as $|A|$, $|M|$ and $|P|$, respectively. As the nonparallel data is abundant but the parallel data is limited, size $|A|, |M| \gg |P|$. The main objective is to convert the input ancient Chinese text a to its modern variant m. This task is akin to style transfer, or if the text are drastically different, machine translation. In this paper, we are only concerned with the direction from zh-a to zh-m. Additionally, we include the prediction of the chronological period of the ancient text as an auxiliary task.

4   Proposed Framework

Our framework translates the given ancient Chinese text (§4.1) while providing additional chronological context information (§4.2) (see Table 1). We train the *translation model* in a semi-supervised manner such that cheap and easy-to-obtain modern Chinese text can be utilized in the training process. To better select from the pool of generated candidates in a time-aware way, we use the multi-label prediction model as both the *reranker* and the *chronology predictor*. The predicted chronological period also provides users with crucial context for understanding the ancient text.

4.1   Semi-Supervised Translation Model

Our sequence-to-sequence model is based on the Transformer (Vaswani et al., 2017) encoder-decoder architecture. Given an input, the encoder first converts it into an intermediate vector, and then the decoder takes the intermediate representation as input to generate a target output. In what follows, we describe the training objectives that allows the translation model to utilize augmented monolingual data.

Semi-Supervised Objectives. Inspired by the previous work on CycleGANs (Zhu et al., 2017) and dual learning (He et al., 2016; Chang et al., 2021a,b), our method trains the initial model in both forward and backward directions, and defines a semi-supervised optimization objective that combines direct supervision ($L_{supervised}$) and a language model loss (L_{lm}) over the parallel data P, and two monolingual corpora A and M:

$$L = L_{supervised}(P) + L_{lm}(A) + L_{lm}(M)$$

where $L_{supervised}(P)$ utilizes the aligned sentence pairs in P to perform domain alignment, ensuring that the representation of the ancient Chinese text can be semantically aligned with its modern variant. Moreover, *the semi-supervised training allows us to augment monolingual modern Chinese for language modeling.* Empirically, we found that this

	Text	Chronological Period
Source (Ancient Chinese)	孟子曰：道在尔而求诸远，事在易而求之难。	pre-qin
Reference	孟子说：道路在近旁而偏要向远处去寻求，事情本来很容易而偏要向难处下手。(Menzie said: "The right path is just beside but people take far away ones instead; things are easy but people handle them with difficult ways.")	
System (Modern Chinese)	孟子说：道理在于尔而求得远方，事情在于易而求得难。	pre-qin
Source (Ancient Chinese)	秦昭王召见，与语，大说之，拜为客卿。	han
Reference	秦昭王便召见了蔡泽。跟他谈话后，很喜欢他，授给他客卿职位。(The King of Qin summoned Mr. Ze Cai and, after talking to him, liked him and gave him a government official position for foreigners.)	
System (Modern Chinese)	秦昭王召见他，与他谈话，非常高兴，拜他为客卿。	han
Source (Ancient Chinese)	太子曰：吾君老矣，非骊姬，寝不安，食不甘。	han
Reference	太子说：我父亲年老了，没有骊姬将睡不稳、食无味。(The Prince said: "My father is old. Without this girl, Li, he cannot sleep well or eat well.")	
System (Modern Chinese)	太子说：我国君已经老了，不是骊姬的姬妾，吃不甘。	han

Table 1: Examples of system output consisting of the *ancient Chinese source*, *modern Chinese reference* and the *chronological period prediction*.

benefits the forward translation from zh-a to zh-m and proves to be a viable way for improving the system.

4.2 Multi-Label Prediction

Further, we improve upon the translation model via the use of the *chronology inference* and *translation reranking* via the dual-purpose *multi-label prediction model*. Specifically, we pretrain a modern Chinese language model then fine-tune this model in a task-specific manner to help predicting the chronological period and using it to also rank the translation model's predictions.

Chronology Inference. To do so, we first pretrain a large-scale language model on the monolingual modern Chinese corpus following objectives in Radford et al. (2019) for GPT-2. This enables the model to be familiarized with the language semantics where some of which are transferrable to the ancient text. Next, we continue to train the GPT-2 model to perform conditional task-specific generation by maximizing the joint probability $p_{\text{GPT-2}}(a, m, c)$, where a is the ancient Chinese text, m is the modern Chinese text, and c represents the contextual information as the chronological period of the ancient text. Specifically, for each sentence pair, the ancient Chinese tokens w_i^a, the modern Chinese tokens w_j^m, and the chronological period are concatenated into "[zh_a] $w_1^a \cdots w_{|a|}^a$ [zh_m] $w_1^m \cdots w_{|m|}^m$ [chron] c", and the model is trained to maximize the probability of this sequence.

Quality Estimation for Reranking. At inference time, we append each of the chronology labels to the translation outputs, then allow the multi-label prediction model to predict their qualities. Specifically, the fine-tuned LM computes the negative log loss on each of the triplets (a, m', c') from the upstream *translation model* by appending *exhaustively* all possible *chronology labels* c' to the end of the generated sequence m' following the same format as above and selecting the best.

5 Dataset Construction

We obtain parallel ancient-modern Chinese sentence pairs, and nonparallel ancient (zh-a) and modern Chinese (zh-m) sentences from two sources (Liu et al., 2019; Shang et al., 2019). Table 2 summarizes the data we used for the experiments.

Chronology Annotation. In this paper, we focus on translating ancient prose. There are a total of 28,807 ancient Chinese prose sentences. We annotate each of these sentences with the Chinese historical period (dynasty) in which it was written. Specifically, we consider three chronology labels: pre-qin (先秦), han (汉), and song (宋). The annotation is based on the source of the sentences, i.e., which ancient book the sentences are taken from. The total number of annotated sentences for each period is 1,244, 20,460, and 7,103 respectively. This annotation scheme can be adopted for a larger set of periods when ancient text of a wider time span is available.

Parallel Data. For the sentences with chronology annotation, we randomly assign 10% sentences to the development set and test set respectively. The

		# sentences	# characters
Nonparallel	zh-a	269,409	4M
	zh-m	77,687	826K
Parallel	Train	27,807	(524K, 797K)
	Dev	2,880	(59K, 88K)
	Test	2,880	(60K, 90K)

Table 2: Statistics of the dataset. For each part of the dataset, the number of sentences and the (source, target) number of characters are shown.

Training Objectives	All	pre-qin	han	song
$L_{supervised}$ (Liu et al., 2019)	19.59	14.41	**20.02**	19.13
$L_{supervised} + L_{lm}(M)$	23.05	15.97	**23.32**	23.17
$L_{supervised} + L_{lm}(M) + L_{lm}(A)$	23.15	14.15	23.34	**23.72**
+ share decoder embeddings	24.38	15.70	24.52	**24.99**
+ time-aware reranking	**24.51**	15.50	24.62	**25.24**

Table 3: Ancient to modern Chinese translation performance. BLEU scores are calculated with 1 to 4 character n-grams.

Period (# test)	Precision	Recall	F1
pre-qin (117)	0.05	0.53	0.09
han (2043)	0.85	0.57	0.68
song (720)	0.85	0.27	0.41
Accuracy			0.49
Macro avg.	0.58	0.45	0.39
Weighted avg.	0.82	0.49	0.59

Table 4: Performance of Chronology Inference

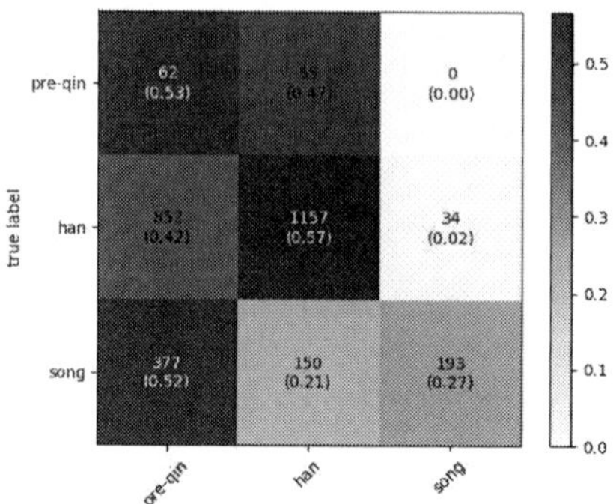

Figure 1: Confusion matrix for Chronology Inference

remaining sentences are used as training data. We further supplement the parallel training data with 4,760 sentences from ancient Chinese poems, each also with a modern Chinese translation. The final training, development and test set statistics and be found in Table 2.

Nonparallel Data. We extend the source-side data by including 269,409 more ancient poem sentences without translation. For extending target-side data, we add 77,687 sentences from modern lyrics, following Shang et al. (2019). The details of nonparallel data are also shown in Table 2.

6 Experimental Settings

We tokenized both ancient and modern Chinese text by splitting characters. The vocabulary sizes are 4,824 and 4,600 respectively. We built our model upon the Fairseq toolkit[3]. The architecture is Transformer with about 54M parameters, which largely follows the configuration of Liu et al. (2019). Translations were generated with beam size 5, and we consider top 5 candidates for reranking. For the *multi-label prediction model*, we adapted existing code[4] to build a GPT-2 Language Model reranker with approximately 82M parameters. First, we pre-trained the model with 1.2 GB of Chinese Wikipedia text. Then, we fine-tuned the pre-trained model with the chronologically-annotated training data. For each ancient-modern sentence pair with chronology information, we

---

[3] https://github.com/pytorch/fairseq
[4] https://github.com/Morizeyao/GPT2-Chinese

form a text-period query string with the scheme described in §4.2. We select the final model according to perplexity computed on the development set.

7 Main Results

Overall, we observe from Table 3 and 4 that the use of the multi-label prediction model not only allows for better context than pure translation, but also helps to boost the general performance on the translation tasks. Moreover, *translations of ancient text chronologically closer to modern Chinese (han and song) tend to yield better performances, as the semantic gaps are generally smaller.* We also demonstrate that the semi-supervised training which avail of the additional nonparallel text helps to improve the translation model even further. Specifically, zh-m nonparallel data enhances the decoder's ability to generate modern Chinese, while zh-a nonparallel data may help the encoder to maintain crucial semantic information. We achieved a BLEU score of 23.15 in this setting. As the source and target side vocabularies have a large overlap, we experimented with sharing decoder embeddings and got +1.23 BLEU improvement, which may also serve as an evidence that there are still ancient components in modern Chinese. Finally, reranking further boosted the BLEU score to 24.51.

Error Analysis. We perform *human evaluation* on 100 randomly sampled output instances and observe them to be high in *adequacy* and *fluency*, 4.06 and 3.68 respectively, on a scale of 0-5. This was done by averaging the fluency and adequacy ratings of three domain experts. Further, we also observe that the chronology of text impacts the model performance as in Table 3. Leveraging zh-m nonparallel data is most helpful for translating text from the `song` period, which is much closer to modern Chinese compared to the text from the other two periods. Further, from Figure 1 we observe that the chronology inference depends very much on the *data scarcity* and the *closeness* of chronological periods. On the Chinese historical timeline, `han` is very close to `pre-qin`, but `han` and `song` are more separated. Another source of difficulty is that ancient Chinese writings tend to quote a considerable amount of text written in previous time periods. For example, a history book written in the `song` period may inherit narratives written in `pre-qin` and `han` for the history before `han`. As a result, it is challenging to perform chronology inference based solely on the linguistic properties of individual sentences. Nevertheless, chronological inference can still provide useful signals for the translation model to better capture semantic differences across time.

8   Conclusion

In this paper, we present a framework that translates ancient Chinese texts into its modern correspondence in low resource scenarios with very little parallel data and a larger set of nonparallel sentences without ancient-modern alignment information. We display the importance and usefulness of chronology inference as an auxiliary task that hints at potential diachronic semantic gaps. We hope to extend this research to further model additional contextual information about each era.

Acknowledgements

This research was funded in part by the German Research Foundation (DFG) as part of SFB 248 "Foundations of Perspicuous Software Systems". We sincerely thank the anonymous reviewers for their insightful comments that helped us to improve this paper.

References

LI Bao-chuan. 2008. Illustrations of antique meanings of the chinese phrases. *Journal of Radio & TV University (Philosophy & Social Sciences)*, 3.

Ernie Chang, Jeriah Caplinger, Alex Marin, Xiaoyu Shen, and Vera Demberg. 2020. Dart: A lightweight quality-suggestive data-to-text annotation tool. *arXiv preprint arXiv:2010.04141*.

Ernie Chang, Vera Demberg, and Alex Marin. 2021a. Jointly improving language understanding and generation with quality-weighted weak supervision of automatic labeling. *Proceedings of EACL 2021*.

Ernie Chang, Xiaoyu Shen, Dawei Zhu, Vera Demberg, and Hui. Su. 2021b. Neural data-to-text generation with lm-based text augmentation. *Proceedings of EACL 2021*.

Ernie Chang, Hui-Syuan Yeh, and Vera Demberg. 2021c. Does the order of training samples matter? improving neural data-to-text generation with curriculum learning. *Proceedings of EACL 2021*.

Di He, Yingce Xia, Tao Qin, Liwei Wang, Nenghai Yu, Tie-Yan Liu, and Wei-Ying Ma. 2016. Dual learning for machine translation. In *Advances in Neural Information Processing Systems*, pages 820–828.

Zhiting Hu, Zichao Yang, Xiaodan Liang, Ruslan Salakhutdinov, and Eric P Xing. 2017. Toward controlled generation of text. In *Proceedings of the 34th International Conference on Machine Learning-Volume 70*, pages 1587–1596. JMLR. org.

Zhijing Jin, Di Jin, Jonas Mueller, Nicholas Matthews, and Enrico Santus. 2019. Unsupervised text style transfer via iterative matching and translation. *arXiv preprint arXiv:1901.11333*.

Dayiheng Liu, Kexin Yang, Qian Qu, and Jiancheng Lv. 2019. Ancient–modern chinese translation with a new large training dataset. *ACM Transactions on Asian and Low-Resource Language Information Processing (TALLIP)*, 19(1):1–13.

Yu Liu. 2019. 现代汉语常用文言虚词的语块教学 [formulaic language instruction of classical grammatical words in modern chinese]. *Chinese as a Second Language. The journal of the Chinese Language Teachers Association, USA*, 54(2):122–144.

Chanjun Park, Chanhee Lee, Yeongwook Yang, and Heuiseok Lim. 2020. Ancient korean neural machine translation. *IEEE Access*, 8:116617–116625.

Shrimai Prabhumoye, Yulia Tsvetkov, Ruslan Salakhutdinov, and Alan W Black. 2018. Style transfer through back-translation. In *Proceedings of the 56th Annual Meeting of the Association for Computational Linguistics (Volume 1: Long Papers)*, pages 866–876. Association for Computational Linguistics.

Alec Radford, Jeffrey Wu, Rewon Child, David Luan, Dario Amodei, and Ilya Sutskever. 2019. Language models are unsupervised multitask learners. *OpenAI Blog*, 1(8).

Sudha Rao and Joel Tetreault. 2018. Dear sir or madam, may i introduce the gyafc dataset: Corpus, benchmarks and metrics for formality style transfer. In *Proceedings of the 2018 Conference of the North American Chapter of the Association for Computational Linguistics: Human Language Technologies, Volume 1 (Long Papers)*, pages 129–140. Association for Computational Linguistics.

Mingyue Shang, Piji Li, Zhenxin Fu, Lidong Bing, Dongyan Zhao, Shuming Shi, and Rui Yan. 2019. Semi-supervised text style transfer: Cross projection in latent space. In *Proceedings of the 2019 Conference on Empirical Methods in Natural Language Processing and the 9th International Joint Conference on Natural Language Processing (EMNLP-IJCNLP)*, pages 4937–4946, Hong Kong, China. Association for Computational Linguistics.

Tianxiao Shen, Tao Lei, Regina Barzilay, and Tommi Jaakkola. 2017. Style transfer from non-parallel text by cross-alignment. In *Advances in neural information processing systems*, pages 6830–6841.

Ashish Vaswani, Noam Shazeer, Niki Parmar, Jakob Uszkoreit, Llion Jones, Aidan N Gomez, Łukasz Kaiser, and Illia Polosukhin. 2017. Attention is all you need. In *Advances in neural information processing systems*, pages 5998–6008.

Zhiyuan Zhang, Wei Li, and Xu Sun. 2018. Automatic transferring between ancient chinese and contemporary chinese. *arXiv preprint arXiv:1803.01557*.

Jun-Yan Zhu, Taesung Park, Phillip Isola, and Alexei A Efros. 2017. Unpaired image-to-image translation using cycle-consistent adversarial networks. In *Proceedings of the IEEE international conference on computer vision*, pages 2223–2232.

Three-part diachronic semantic change dataset for Russian

Andrey Kutuzov
University of Oslo
Norway
andreku@ifi.uio.no

Lidia Pivovarova
University of Helsinki
Finland
lidia.pivovarova@helsinki.fi

Abstract

We present a manually annotated lexical semantic change dataset for Russian: RuShiftEval. Its novelty is ensured by a single set of target words annotated for their diachronic semantic shifts across three time periods, while the previous work either used only two time periods, or different sets of target words. The paper describes the composition and annotation procedure for the dataset. In addition, it is shown how the ternary nature of RuShiftEval allows to trace specific diachronic trajectories: 'changed at a particular time period and stable afterwards' or 'was changing throughout all time periods'. Based on the analysis of the submissions to the recent shared task on semantic change detection for Russian, we argue that correctly identifying such trajectories can be an interesting sub-task itself.

1 Introduction

This paper describes *RuShiftEval*: a new dataset of diachronic semantic changes for Russian words. Its novelty in comparison with prior work is its multi-period nature. Until now, semantic change detection datasets focused on shifts occurring between **two** time periods. On the other hand, *RuShiftEval* provides human-annotated degrees of semantic change for a set of Russian nouns over **three** time periods: pre-Soviet (1700-1916), Soviet (1918-1990) and post-Soviet (1992-2016). Notably, it also contains 'skipping' comparisons of pre-Soviet meanings versus post-Soviet meanings. Together, this forms three subsets: *RuShiftEval*-1 (pre-Soviet VS Soviet), *RuShiftEval*-2 (Soviet VS post-Soviet) and *RuShiftEval*-3 (pre-Soviet VS post-Soviet).

The three periods naturally stem from the Russian history: they were radically different in terms of life realities and writing and practices, which is reflected in the language. As an example, the word дядька lost its 'tutor of a kid in a rich family'

sense in the Soviet times, with only the generic 'adult man' sense remaining. Certainly, language development never stops and Russian also gradually evolved within those periods as well, not only on their boundaries. However, in order to create a usable semantic change dataset, one has to draw the boundaries somewhere, and it is difficult to come up with more fitting 'changing points' for Russian.

RuShiftEval can be used for testing the ability of semantic change detection systems to trace long-term multi-point dynamics of diachronic semantic shifts, rather than singular change values measured by comparing two time periods. As such, *RuShiftEval* was successfully employed in a recent shared task on semantic change detection for Russian (Kutuzov and Pivovarova, 2021).

2 Related work

Automatic detection of word meaning change is a fast growing research area (Kutuzov et al., 2018; Tahmasebi et al., 2018). Evaluation of this task is especially challenging; *inter alia*, it requires gold standard annotation covering multiple word usages.

The common practice is to annotate pairs of sentences as using a target word in either the same or different senses. It was introduced for the word sense disambiguation task in (Erk et al., 2013), while (Schlechtweg et al., 2018) proposed methods to aggregate pairwise annotations for semantic change modeling; one of them, the COMPARE metrics, is used in *RuShiftEval*.

A similar approach was used for the SemEval'20 shared task on semantic change detection (Schlechtweg et al., 2020): annotators labeled pairs of sentences, where some pairs belonged to the same periods and some to different ones. This annotation resulted in a diachronic word usage graph, which was then clustered to obtain sepa-

Proceedings of the 2nd International Workshop on Computational Approaches to Historical Language Change 2021, pages 7–13
August 6, 2021. ©2021 Association for Computational Linguistics

rate word senses and their distributions between time periods (Schlechtweg et al., 2021).

The pairwise sentence annotation has been used in creating another semantic change dataset for Russian, *RuSemShift* (Rodina and Kutuzov, 2020). We use the same annotation procedure and rely on the same corpus, i.e. Russian National Corpus (RNC) split into pre-Soviet, Soviet and post-Soviet subcorpora. However, *RuSemShift* features two sets of words: one for the changes between the pre-Soviet and Soviet periods, and another for the Soviet and post-Soviet periods. The new *RuShiftEval* dataset, which we present in this paper, uses a *joint word set* allowing for tracing each word across three time periods. In addition, we directly annotate semantic change between the pre-Soviet and post-Soviet periods, skipping the Soviet one.

3 Dataset Construction

3.1 Word List Creation

In building the dataset, we relied on the graded view on word meaning change (Schlechtweg et al., 2021): for each word in the dataset, we measure a *degree of change* between pairs of periods, rather than making a binary decision on whether its sense inventory changed over time. The measure relies on pairwise sentence annotations, where each pair of sentences is processed by at least three annotators.

Compiling the target-word set, we needed to ensure two main conditions: (i) the dataset contains many 'interesting' words, i.e. words that changed their meaning between either pair of periods; (ii) not all words in the dataset actually changed their meaning. We followed the same procedure as in (Kutuzov and Kuzmenko, 2018; Rodina and Kutuzov, 2020; Schlechtweg et al., 2020): first, select changing words, and then augment them with *fillers*, i.e. random words following similar frequency distribution across three time periods.

Technically, it was possible to populate the target word set automatically, using any pre-trained language model (LM) for Russian and some measure of distance between word representations in different corpora. However, we wanted our target words choice to be motivated linguistically rather than influenced by any LM architecture. Therefore, to find changing words, we first consulted several dictionaries of outdated or, on the contrary, the most recent Russian words, such as (Novikov, 2016; Basko and Andreeva, 2011; Skljarevsky, 1998). Unfortunately, dictionaries provided less examples than we

needed: they often contain archaisms, neologisms, multi-word expressions, and words which are infrequent in the corpus or not used in the meanings specified in the dictionaries.

However, we discovered that some changing words could be found in papers on specific linguistics problems. For example, the word облако ('cloud') was found in a paper on the Internet language (Baldanova and Stepanova, 2016); стол ('table/diet')—in an article discussing the language of one story by Pushkin (M., 2016). Finally, to find some of the target words, we used our intuition as educated native speakers. Out of 50 words, 13 were found in dictionaries, 10 invented by ourselves and the rest 27 found in articles on more specific topics. Regardless the initial word origin, we manually checked that all words occur at least 50 times in each of the three sub-corpora and that the distinctive sense is used several times.

Fillers (selected for each target word) are sampled so that they belong to the same part of speech—nouns in our case—and their frequency percentile is the same as the target word frequency percentile in all three periods. The aim here is to ensure that frequency cannot be used to distinguish the target words from fillers.[1] For *RuShiftEval*, we sampled two filler words for each target word.

The final dataset consists of 111 Russian nouns, where 12 words form a development set and 99 words serve as a test set. Since the annotation procedure is the same as for *RuSemShift* (Rodina and Kutuzov, 2020), one can use one of these resources as a training set and then evaluate on another.

3.2 Annotation

Annotators' guidelines were identical to those in *RuSemShift* (Rodina and Kutuzov, 2020). To generate annotation tasks, we sampled 30 sentences from each sub-corpus and created sentence pairs. We ran this sampling independently for all three period pairs. The sentences were accompanied by one preceding and one following sentence, to ease the annotators' work in case of doubt. The task was formulated as labeling on a 1-4 scale, where 1 means the senses of the target word in two sentences are unrelated, 2 stands for 'distantly related', 3 stands for 'closely related', and 4 stands for 'senses are identical' (Hätty et al., 2019). Annotators were also allowed to use the 0 ('cannot decide') judgments.

---

[1] Indeed, there is no significant correlation between frequency differences and the aggregated relatedness scores from our gold annotation.

Time bins	α	ρ	**JUD**	**0-JUD**
Test set (99 words)				
RuShiftEval-1	0.506	0.521	8 863	42
RuShiftEval-2	0.549	0.559	8 879	25
RuShiftEval-3	0.544	0.556	8 876	31
Development set (12 words)				
RuShiftEval-1	0.592	0.613	1 013	7
RuShiftEval-2	0.609	0.627	1 014	3
RuShiftEval-3	0.597	0.632	1 015	2

Table 1: *RuShiftEval* statistics. α and ρ are inter-rater agreement scores as calculated by Krippendorff's α (ordinal scale) and mean pairwise Spearman ρ. JUD is total number of judgments and 0-JUD is the number of 0-judgments ('cannot decide').

They were excluded from the final datasets, but their number was negligible anyway: about 100 out of total 30 000.

The annotation was carried out on the Yandex.Toloka crowd-sourcing platform.[2] We employed native speakers of Russian, older than 30, with a university degree. To ensure the annotation quality, the authors themselves annotated about 20 control examples for each pair of periods. We chose the most obvious cases of 1 and 4 for this; annotators who answered incorrectly (not with the exactly matching grade), were banned from the task for 24 hours. The inter-rater agreement statistics and the number of judgments in each *RuShiftEval* subset are shown in Table 1. The agreement is on par with other semantic change annotation efforts: (Schlechtweg et al., 2020) report Spearman correlations ranging from 0.58 to 0.69, (Rodina and Kutuzov, 2020) report Krippendorff's α ranging from 0.51 to 0.53.[3] Each subset was annotated by about 100 human raters, more or less uniformly 'spread' across annotation instances, with the only constraint being that each instance must be annotated by three different persons.

Finally, the degrees of semantic change for each word between a pair of periods were calculated using the COMPARE metrics (Schlechtweg et al., 2018), which is the average of pairwise relatedness scores. Interestingly, some words initially sampled as fillers—e.g. ядро ('cannonball or core/nucleus')—ended up among most changed according to the annotation. Also some words from the initial set were annotated as relatively stable. This happened because the distinctive sense was rare or because annotators' opinion diverged from linguistic knowledge in the dictionaries. For example, for the word бригада ('brigade/gang/team') dictionaries list two distinct senses—a military and a civil one. However, in most cases the annotators considered these senses identical or closely related.

The dataset is publicly available, including the raw scores assigned by annotators.[4]

4 Diachronic trajectory types

RuShiftEval allows tracing multi-hop dynamics of semantic change. A similar analysis of diachronic word embedding series or 'trajectories' was conducted in (Kulkarni et al., 2015) and (Hamilton et al., 2016b), but the former focused on change point detection, and the latter on finding general laws of semantic change. With manually annotated *RuShiftEval* dataset we were able to move further and identify at least three different types of changing trajectories: 1) changes in every period pair; 2) change in the Soviet period as compared to the pre-Soviet period; 3) change in the post-Soviet period as compared to the Soviet period.

Since approximately a half of the words in the dataset did not change their meaning they exhibit a fourth, trivial type of trajectory, where all three distances are small. In principle there could be a fifth type of trajectory, where difference between pre-Soviet and post-Soviet periods is substantially smaller than between other period pairs, which would mean that a word was used in a new sense during the Soviet time but then came back to its original meaning. However, we did not find any words following this trajectory type and not sure whether this behavior is theoretically plausible.

Table 2 shows examples of nouns belonging to three non-stable trajectory types. Below we explain the semantic change processes for them.

1. The word закладка belongs to the type 1. Its dominant sense in the pre-Soviet period was 'foundation' (as in '*The foundation of the new church building took place yesterday*'). In the Soviet times, the 'bookmark' sense emerged (it was already present before, but very rare). Then, the post-Soviet time period saw the emergence of two

---

[2] https://toloka.yandex.ru/

[3] Note it does not make much sense to report correlations for individual annotators ('data columns'), since in our crowd-working setup, the columns are not associated with particular persons.

[4] https://github.com/akutuzov/rushifteval_public

Type	Examples	Baseline	Top
1	закладка ('foundation/bookmark/hidden artifact'), линейка ('carriage/ruler/series of goods'), центр ('center')	0.5	1.0
2	дядька ('tutor/adult man'), живот ('life/belly/stomach'), лох ('salmon/silver-berry/easy victim, stupid person'), роспись ('list/painting'), ядро ('cannonball/core/nucleus')	1.0	1.0
3	полоса ('stripe/ribbon/lane/runway'), связка ('ligament/vocal cords/mutual connection'), спутник ('fellow traveler/satellite/sputnik'), ссылка ('exile/link'), тачка ('wheelbarrow/car'), формат ('format')	0.4	0.8-1.0

Table 2: Semantic change trajectory types in *RuShiftEval* and the percentage of words with correctly captured type for the baseline and the 4 best shared task submissions (see 4.1).

new senses, both through widening processes: 'tab' (in graphical user interfaces) and 'booby-trapping' or 'something hidden' (often about illegal drugs cached by a distributor). Thus, low relatedness scores are observed across all possible pairs: the word is used differently in each time period.

2. The word ядро can mean either 'cannonball' or 'core/kernel/nucleus'. It belongs to the type 2. In the Soviet period, the first sense almost disappeared (because artillery stopped using cannonballs in the 20th century), while the latter sense became more frequent. After this reduction, the meaning was stable, with no changes in the post-Soviet period.

3. The word тачка ('wheelbarrow') belongs to the type 3. It was stable until the end of the Soviet period, but in the post-Soviet times, тачка acquired a new colloquial sense of 'car', quite common even in written texts. This lead to divergence from both Soviet and pre-Soviet periods.

Semantic trajectory types could be visualized as time relatedness graphs; see Figure 1. Nodes of the graph are time periods, and edge widths represent the COMPARE score (see 3.2) for each pair of periods.[5] Thus, thicker edges denote stable meaning, while thinner and more transparent edges show a change. Each trajectory type has its own characteristic pattern of edge widths. For example, in the graph for тачка (the rightmost plot), the edges connecting the post-Soviet node to two other nodes are much thinner than the edge between the pre-Soviet and post-Soviet nodes. This signals a change in the post-Soviet times (trajectory type 3).

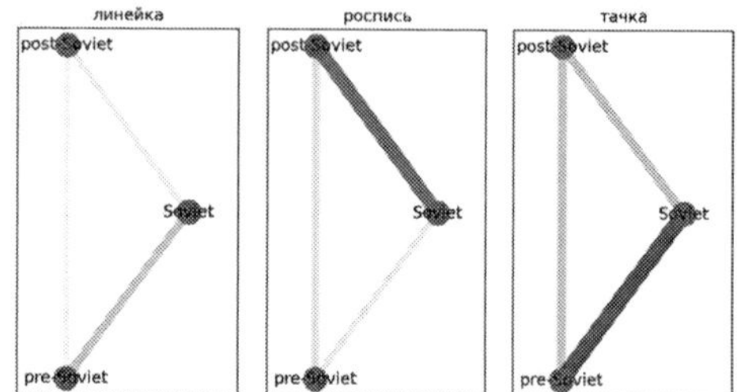

Figure 1: Time relatedness graphs for words belonging to different semantic trajectory types (from left to right): линейка ('carriage/ruler/series of goods') (1), роспись ('list/painting') (2), тачка ('wheelbarrow/car') (3).

Note that the annotation process and the definition of the COMPARE score itself do not guarantee perfect capturing of semantic changes. One example—made clear by the multi-period nature of *RuShiftEval* design—is the word радикал ('radical'). Its relatedness scores are low across all time period pairs, suggesting that it experienced sequential changes similar to закладка. However, in fact, throughout all the times covered by *RuShiftEval*, this word had the same two persistent senses: political and chemical. Since their probabilities were almost equal, many randomly sampled sentence pairs contained the word радикал in two different senses, which led to low COMPARE scores. In this case, it stems from strong and persistent ambiguity of the word, not from diachronic semantic change. This limitation of the COMPARE metrics was already described in (Schlechtweg et al., 2018).

Another potential flaw is sampling variability. For annotation, we sampled 30 sentences with a target word from each time period for each comparison. Since our relatedness graph has three edges,

---

[5]Note that in most cases it is impossible to use nodes relative positions on the plot to reflect relatedness scores: one can't change the length of an edge in a triangle without also changing the length of at least one other edge.

each word is represented with two samples. As it turned out, in some cases different samples can yield quite different picture of sense distributions.

Let us manually analyze the word полость ('cavity/hide to cover one's legs in an open cart'). Since horse-driven carts disappeared just a few years after the beginning of the Soviet period, one might expect the second sense to be lost in Soviet times and never to appear again. However, the relatedness between the Soviet and post-Soviet time periods (1.9) is even lower than between the pre-Soviet and Soviet periods (2.2), as if the word experienced another semantic shift. In fact, it is a random sampling artifact. In the 30 sentences from the Soviet period sampled for the 'pre-Soviet:Soviet' pair, only 4 used полость in this archaic sense. But in the 30 sentences *from the same period* sampled for the 'Soviet:post-Soviet' pair, this number grew to 10, 2.5 times more (mostly in fiction texts, where the plot is set in the pre-Soviet times). As a result, the Soviet usage pattern looks like it is different from the post-Soviet one, although in fact no shift has happened (as evident both from linguistic intuition of Russian speakers and from the Fisher exact test which in this case yields $p = 0.13$). The frequency of полость in the Soviet sub-corpus is about 600, so both samples together cover only 10% of the full concordance. Without manually annotating all six hundred occurrences, it is difficult to tell which sample is more representative of the real word usage in the Soviet times. It would be better to increase the sample size as much as possible: 30 is arguably already on the border.

4.1 Trajectory detection task?

The *RuShiftEval* dataset was used to evaluate the systems participating in a shared task on lexical semantic change detection for Russian (Kutuzov and Pivovarova, 2021). How good these submissions are in capturing the trajectory types described in the previous section? In this subsection, we describe a toy experiment to address this question.

For simplicity, we will use only 11 example words from Table 2 which appear in the *RuShiftEval* evaluation set (this excludes закладка, лох and спутник, since they appear in the development set only). Then a set of criteria is established for the system predictions, corresponding to each of the three trajectory types. We consider a system successful in capturing a word with the **trajectory 2** if the predicted relatedness score is higher for the 'Soviet:post-Soviet' pair than for other two pairs. For the words with the **trajectory 3**, the relatedness score for the 'pre-Soviet:Soviet' pair must be the highest among all pairs. For the words with the **trajectory 1**, the percentile ranks of the relatedness scores for all three sub-sets must be below 50 (admittedly, this is an *ad hoc* criterion, but it is used here just to give an example of how the task can be set up). Thus, at least for the trajectory types 2 and 3, this resembles a simple ranking task: not across target words within one period pair, but for one target word across three period pairs. At the same time, the trajectory type 1 (changes in every period) does not quite fit into this frame.

We compared the baseline system (which used static diachronic word embeddings and the local neighbors method from (Hamilton et al., 2016a)) and four best systems (employing contextualized language models: ELMo, BERT or XLM-R). The results are presented in Table 2. All of the best submissions captured the **trajectory 1** for all two target words, but the baseline method failed for центр (its percentile rank in *RuShiftEval*-1 is more than 60). For the **trajectory 3**, the top systems are considerably better than the baseline method. For example, according to the baseline method, полоса experienced its strongest change in the Soviet times, while in fact it was in the post-Soviet period. Only for the **trajectory 2**, the baseline is on par with the winners of the shared task.

This analysis is rather preliminary, but it shows that the systems performance in correctly detecting diachronic trajectories does to some extent correlate with their performance in the 'traditional' semantic change ranking (with binary datasets, like in the SemEval 2020 Shared Task 1). We believe that this can be an interesting sub-task within the larger field of semantic change detection, once more datasets like *RuShiftEval* are available and more formal definitions of 'capturing the trajectory successfully' are developed.

5   Conclusion

We presented *RuShiftEval*, a novel dataset of diachronic semantic changes in Russian nouns across three time periods, using the same set of target words for all comparisons. We also conducted a preliminary analysis of how *RuShiftEval* can be used in tracing diachronic semantic trajectories, and how current change detection systems for Russian deal with this potentially interesting task.

Acknowledgments

The annotation effort for *RuShiftEval* was supported by the Russian Science Foundation grant 20-18-00206. This work has been partially supported by the European Union Horizon 2020 research and innovation programme under grants 770299 (NewsEye) and 825153 (EMBEDDIA).

References

Marina Baldanova and Irina Stepanova. 2016. Metaforizatsiya kak put' razvitiya semanticheskikh neologizmov v yazyke interneta (metaphorization as a way of developing semantic neologisms in the language of the internet). *In Russian.*

Nina Basko and Irina Andreeva. 2011. *Slovar' ustarevshey leksiki k proizvedeniyam russkoy klassiki (Dictionary of obsolete vocabulary for the works of Russian classics).* In Russian.

Katrin Erk, Diana McCarthy, and Nicholas Gaylord. 2013. Measuring word meaning in context. *Computational Linguistics*, 39(3):511–554.

William L. Hamilton, Jure Leskovec, and Dan Jurafsky. 2016a. Cultural shift or linguistic drift? comparing two computational measures of semantic change. In *Proceedings of the 2016 Conference on Empirical Methods in Natural Language Processing*, pages 2116–2121, Austin, Texas. Association for Computational Linguistics.

William L. Hamilton, Jure Leskovec, and Dan Jurafsky. 2016b. Diachronic word embeddings reveal statistical laws of semantic change. In *Proceedings of the 54th Annual Meeting of the Association for Computational Linguistics (Volume 1: Long Papers)*, pages 1489–1501, Berlin, Germany. Association for Computational Linguistics.

Anna Hätty, Dominik Schlechtweg, and Sabine Schulte im Walde. 2019. SURel: A gold standard for incorporating meaning shifts into term extraction. In *Proceedings of the Eighth Joint Conference on Lexical and Computational Semantics (*SEM 2019)*, pages 1–8, Minneapolis, Minnesota. Association for Computational Linguistics.

Vivek Kulkarni, Rami Al-Rfou, Bryan Perozzi, and Steven Skiena. 2015. Statistically significant detection of linguistic change. In *Proceedings of the 24th International Conference on World Wide Web*, pages 625–635, Florence, Italy.

Andrey Kutuzov and Elizaveta Kuzmenko. 2018. Two centuries in two thousand words: neural embedding models in detecting diachronic lexical changes. *Quantitative Approaches to the Russian Language*, page 95.

Andrey Kutuzov, Lilja Øvrelid, Terrence Szymanski, and Erik Velldal. 2018. Diachronic word embeddings and semantic shifts: a survey. In *Proceedings of the 27th International Conference on Computational Linguistics*, pages 1384–1397, Santa Fe, New Mexico, USA. Association for Computational Linguistics.

Andrey Kutuzov and Lidia Pivovarova. 2021. RuShiftEval: a shared task on semantic shift detection for Russian. In print.

Elmi A. M. 2016. Izmeneniya znacheniya odnoznachnykh imen sushchestvitel'nykh, upotreblonnykh v povesti as pushkina "grobovshchik" (changes in the meaning of unambiguous nouns used in as pushkin's story "the undertaker"). *In Russian.*

Vladimir Novikov. 2016. *Dictionary of buzzwords. The linguistic picture of our time.* In Russian.

Julia Rodina and Andrey Kutuzov. 2020. RuSemShift: a dataset of historical lexical semantic change in Russian. In *Proceedings of the 28th International Conference on Computational Linguistics*, pages 1037–1047, Barcelona, Spain (Online). International Committee on Computational Linguistics.

Dominik Schlechtweg, Barbara McGillivray, Simon Hengchen, Haim Dubossarsky, and Nina Tahmasebi. 2020. SemEval-2020 task 1: Unsupervised lexical semantic change detection. In *Proceedings of the Fourteenth Workshop on Semantic Evaluation*, pages 1–23, Barcelona (online). International Committee for Computational Linguistics.

Dominik Schlechtweg, Nina Tahmasebi, Simon Hengchen, Haim Dubossarsky, and Barbara McGillivray. 2021. DWUG: A large resource of diachronic word usage graphs in four languages. *arXiv preprint arXiv:2104.08540.*

Dominik Schlechtweg, Sabine Schulte im Walde, and Stefanie Eckmann. 2018. Diachronic usage relatedness (DURel): A framework for the annotation of lexical semantic change. In *Proceedings of the 2018 Conference of the North American Chapter of the Association for Computational Linguistics: Human Language Technologies, Volume 2 (Short Papers)*, pages 169–174, New Orleans, Louisiana. Association for Computational Linguistics.

Skljarevsky, editor. 1998. *Tolkovyy slovar' russkogo yazyka kontsa XX veka. YAzykovyye izmeneniya. (Explanatory dictionary of the Russian language at the end of the XX century. Language changes).* In Russian.

Nina Tahmasebi, Lars Borin, and Adam Jatowt. 2018. Survey of computational approaches to diachronic conceptual change. *arXiv preprint arXiv:1811.06278.*

A   Transliterations of Russian words mentioned in the article

WORD	TRANSLITERATION	TRANSLATION
бригада	brigada	brigade/gang/team
дядька	djadka	uncle/man/(male) tutor
живот	život	stomach/belly/life
закладка	zakladka	foundation/bookmark/hidden artifact
линейка	lineika	carriage/ruler/series of goods
лох	loh	salmon/silver-berry/easy victim
облако	oblako	cloud
полоса	polosa	tripe/ribbon/lane/runway
полость	polost	cavity/foot hide
радикал	radikal	radical
роспись	rospis	mural/signature/list
связка	svjazka	ligament/vocal cords/mutual connection
спутник	sputnik	fellow traveler/satellite/sputnik
ссылка	ssylka	exile/link
стол	stol	table/diet
тачка	tachka	wheelbarrow/car
формат	format	format
центр	tsentr	center
ядро	jadro	cannonball/core/nucleus

The Corpora They Are a-Changing:
a Case Study in Italian Newspapers

Pierpaolo Basile [a] **Annalina Caputo** [b], **Tommaso Caselli** [c],
Pierluigi Cassotti [a], **Rossella Varvara** [d]

[a] Dept. of Computer Science, University of Bari
[b] ADAPT Centre School of Computing, Dublin City University
[c] CLCG, University of Groningen
[d] Dept. of Computer Science, University of Turin
{pierpaolo.basile,pierluigi.cassotti}@uniba.it
annalina.caputo@dcu.ie, t.caselli@rug.nl
rossella.varvara@unito.it

Abstract

The use of automatic methods for the study of lexical semantic change (LSC) has led to the creation of evaluation benchmarks. Benchmark datasets, however, are intimately tied to the corpus used for their creation questioning their reliability as well as the robustness of automatic methods. This contribution investigates these aspects showing the impact of unforeseen social and cultural dimensions. We also identify a set of additional issues (OCR quality, named entities) that impact the performance of the automatic methods, especially when used to discover LSC.

1 Introduction

Natural languages are *de facto* living entities always subject to change and evolution. The diachronic dimension of natural language has played a pivotal role in the history of Linguistics. Understanding and explaining why a community of speakers "speak" as they do is of primary importance to access one's cultural heritage and perspectives on the world.

In recent years, the Natural Language Processing (NLP) community has developed an interest in historical linguistics, and in particular in the study of lexical semantics change (LSC). Previous work has investigated LSC using different approaches, including statistical tests over time period (Popescu and Strapparava, 2013), supervised methods (Mihalcea and Nastase, 2012), count-based distributional approaches (Gulordava and Baroni, 2011), sense-based methods (Kim et al., 2014; Mitra et al., 2014; Frermann and

Lapata, 2016), and neural language models (Hamilton et al., 2016a,b; Schlechtweg et al., 2018; Orlikowski et al., 2018; Brandl and Lassner, 2019; Gonen et al., 2020; Giulianelli et al., 2020; Schlechtweg et al., 2020). This has been possible thanks to two factors: increased availability of machine-readable texts covering different periods and increased processing capabilities. The use of computational models for studying LSC is not free from problems, however, as highlighted by Hengchen et al. (2021).

Almost every computational model for LSC is grounded on the Distributional Hypothesis of meaning according to which "the meaning of a word is its use" (Wittgenstein, 2010) and the "difference in meaning correlates with difference in distribution" (Harris, 1954). Distributional models are powerful, yet they suffer from some limitations, namely: (i) they require large amount of text; (ii) they are sensitive to the type of texts and the distribution (i.e., frequency) of the lexical items; and (iii) they tend to conflate different types of information and variables such as semantics, social and topical information.

This contribution investigates two strictly connected aspects: the reliability of LSC benchmark data and the sensitivity of a state-of-the-art approach for LSC, grounded on the distributional hypothesis, when changing the source corpus. The results of our work will help to shed light on systems' robustness and stability by verifying whether methods tuned on one corpus can be directly applied to another.

Proceedings of the 2nd International Workshop on Computational Approaches to Historical Language Change 2021, pages 14–20
August 6, 2021. ©2021 Association for Computational Linguistics

2 Methodology

To test benchmark independence and models' robustness for LSC, we design a set of experiments using two source corpora, a common benchmark, and a common architecture for LSC detection.

The first corpus is the "L'Unità" corpus (Basile et al., 2020a). It covers a time span between 1945–2014 and it has been collected, pre-processed, and released for the DIACR-Ita (Diachronic Lexical Semantics in Italian) task (Basile et al., 2020b), a LSC change shared task for Italian. Texts were extracted from PDF files by using the Apache Tika library[1] and pre-processed with spaCy[2] for tokenization, PoS-tagging, lemmatization, named entity recognition and dependency parsing. The second corpus was obtained by crawling a publicly available digital archive of the Italian newspaper "La Stampa". The corpus covers a shorter time period (1945–2005) and it was pre-processed using the same tools and pipeline of "L'Unità". Each corpus is split into two sub-corpora, C_1 and C_2, covering different time periods. Table 1 summarises the basic statistics of corpora and the time periods of each sub-corpus.

Corpus	Subcorpus	Tokens
L'Unità	C_1 [1945 – 1970]	52,287,734
L'Unità	C_2 [1990 – 2014]	196,539,403
La Stampa	C_1 [1945 – 1970]	670,281,513
La Stampa	C_2 [1990 – 2005]	1,193,959,080

Table 1: Corpora statistics.

The corpora present two major differences. First, as shown in Table 1, the number of tokens in "La Stampa" is consistently larger than "L'Unità". Second, the political and social orientations of the two newspapers are different. Historically, "L'Unità" has been the official newspaper of the Italian Communist Party and of its successors PDS/DS. "La Stampa" is the oldest newspaper in Italy, traditionally it has voiced centrist and liberal positions.

The only benchmark for Italian has been proposed in the context of DIACR-Ita. The dataset contains 18 target lemmas, 6 of which are instances of a LSC. The dataset was manually created using the "L'Unità" corpus, where a valid LSC corresponds to the acquisition of a new meaning by a target word in C_2.

[1] https://tika.apache.org/
[2] https://spacy.io/

As architecture for automatic LSC detection, we obtain comparable diachronic representations of word meanings by re-implementing the Word2Vec Skipgram model (Mikolov et al., 2013) with Orthogonal Procrustes (OP-SGNS) (Hamilton et al., 2016b). In particular, we adopted the implementation proposed by Kaiser et al. (2020), a state-of-the-art system that ranked 1st both at DIACR-Ita and at SemEval 2020 Task 1: Unsupervised Lexical Semantic Change Detection (Schlechtweg et al., 2020). Model parameters are reported in Appendix A. Word embeddings were generated using lemmas to reduce sparseness and facilitate the evaluation against the benchmark.

3 Testing for Robustness and Independence

Testing for robustness and consistency for LSC is not trivial since it requires to distinguish between two strictly connected dimensions: (i) reliability of the benchmark (dataset dimension), and (ii) variations in data distributions (corpora dimension). The first dimension (dataset) is analysed by comparing on the DIACR-Ita benchmark the performances of the same model trained on the two corpora. The corpora dimension is investigated by manually inspecting the disagreements between the model predictions. All 18 target words in the benchmark satisfy a minimal frequency threshold of 10 both in C_1 and C_2 in "La Stampa", allowing us to reliably compare the results.

To study the reliability of the DIACR-Ita benchmark with respect to the underlying corpus, for each target word in the benchmark, we computed the cosine similarity of its embedding representation from each sub-corpus (C_1 and C_2). To account for the random initialisation of the OP-SGNS parameters, we ran 10 experiments with different initialisations and averaged the results. The system accuracy is computed as the fraction of correctly predicted words over the total number of words in the benchmark. A target word is deemed as an instance of LSC when its cosine similarity across the two time periods is below a given threshold λ^*.

Since the focus is on the reliability of the benchmark across corpora, and not the system performances, the threshold λ^* for each corpus is set up to the value that maximises the system performance on the corpus.

Using the optimal threshold, our implementation of OP-SGNS obtained an accuracy of $0.96 \pm .02$

when trained on "L'Unità" and $0.83 \pm .00$ when trained on "La Stampa", a difference spawned by the incorrect classification of the words *ape* (LSC), *rampante* (LSC), and *brama* (stable).

To understand the role of the two corpora, we compare the target word similarities between C_1 and C_2 on the two corpora. Figure 1a and Figure 1b illustrate the similarities of the stable and LSC target words, respectively. Overall, the identification of LSC target words seems consistent among the two corpora, and lets us assume that the benchmark is reliable and the algorithm is robust.

We further analyse the system's disagreements by manually exploring their occurrences in each corpus for every time period.[3] For the target *brama* ('yearning'), "La Stampa" indicates a potential LSC. The manual inspection, however, has confirmed the annotation in the benchmark (i.e., a stable meaning) showing that the change is triggered by the presence of this word in band names in the C_2 portion of the corpus. *Ape* ('bee') is listed in the benchmark as an LCS, since in C_2 it refers not only to the insect, but also to a three-wheeled vehicle. Despite this new sense is present in the C_2 sub-corpus of "La Stampa", the difference in similarity is above the threshold. Interestingly, in this corpus we observe the three-wheeled vehicle sense also in C_1, especially as part of paid advertisements. This points to a bias in the corpus (i.e, "L'Unità") used to create the benchmark, namely the lack of (or extremely limited) presence of advertisements, which has obfuscated the occurrence of the three-wheeled vehicle sense and suggested *ape* as a good candidate for an LSC. *Ape* is interesting also for another reason: the discrepancy between when it was first on the market (1948) and its first attestation in the Sabatini Coletti dictionary (1983). Further related to the more commercial nature of the "La Stampa" newspaper is the higher difference in similarity with respect to the "L'Unità" for the word *rampante* ('rampant'/'high-flying'). In "La Stampa", the word occurs also in C_1 as part of the book title "Il barone rampante"; this has mitigated the variation in context of usage with the occurrences of *rampante* in C_2.

4   Models into the Wild

We further extended the analysis to the whole common vocabulary of the two corpora to test the ro-

bustness of the computational model. In particular, we consider the vocabulary intersection V of the two sub-corpora, that consists of 48,681 lemmas. Then, we compute the two sets X and Y of cosine similarities for all the words in V. A first analysis was conducted to understand to which extent the rank order of the two sets X and Y are correlated. The Spearman Correlation between the two sets is 0.67 (p-value < 0.01), which indicates a positive correlation between the two rank orders, suggesting that the output of OP-SGNS is similar across the two corpora. The plots of the correlations are reported in Figure 2 in Appendix B.

In this analysis, the optimal thresholds cannot be computed due to the lack of a gold-standard for the whole vocabulary intersection V. Potential LSC instances are identified by using as threshold the difference between the average of the cosine similarities (μ) and the standard deviation (σ) over the set V:

$$LCS(X) = \{t_i \in V \mid x_i < \mu(X) - \sigma(X)\}$$

Where t_i is the term associated with the ith similarity $x_i \in X$. Similarly, we compute the set $LCS(Y)$. The intersection of the two LCS sets consists of 2,283 lemmas. A quick inspection of the proposed LSCs immediately triggers observations concerning two aspects: (i) the well formedness of a lemma; and (ii) the presence of named entities (NEs). By well formedness, we refer to the lemma being an actual word attested in a reference dictionary of Italian. Indeed, some of the lemmas with the lowest similarity scores, e.g., *gaucha, bwa, bill, -anche*, do not appear to be well formed Italian words. Reasons for this are to be found in the quality of the digitized versions of the documents of the two corpora, the presence of foreign words (e.g., *frere*, French for 'brother'), as well as tokenization errors of the pre-processing tool. We use the list of lemmas in the Sabatini Coletti dictionary to filter out all of these entries.

NEs appear to be an additional source of noise. Lemmas like *albertarelli, beraudo, napoleoni, armellini*, are all instances of NEs referring to people's surnames. We automatically filter NEs in two steps: (i) for each word in a sequence tagged as NE by spaCy, we retrieve and store separately the corresponding lemma; (ii) every candidate LSC lemma is matched against the list generated in (i), greedily filtering all lemmas found to be part of a NE.

16

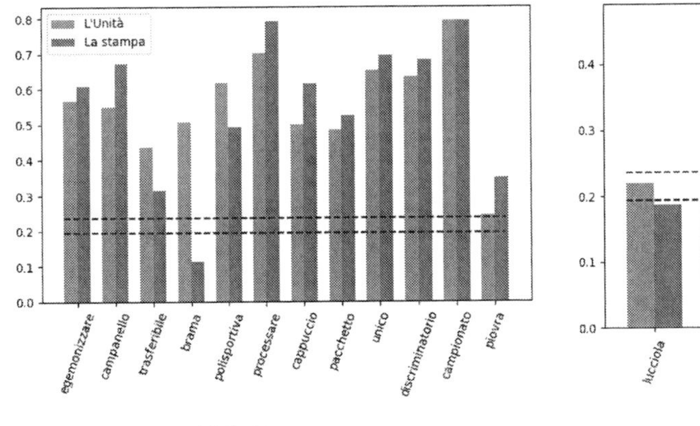
(a) Stable targets.

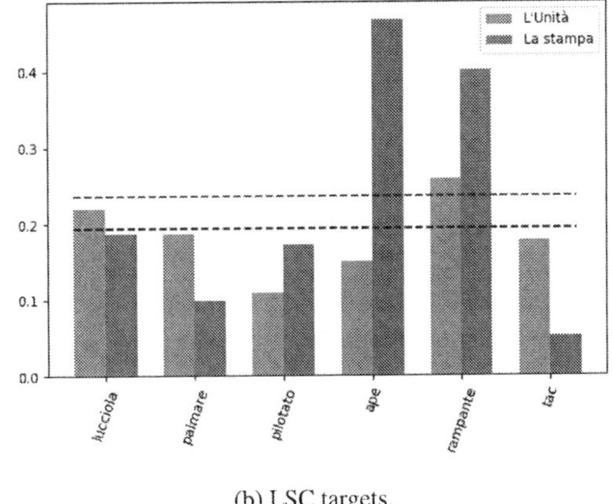
(b) LSC targets.

Figure 1: LSC change scores computed using cosine similarity on both "L'Unità"and "La Stampa"corpus. The dashed lines indicate the λ^* thresholds, computed respectively on "L'Unità"and "La Stampa"corpus. Similarities below the thresholds trigger an LSC.

After the filtering, only 232 lemmas remain. We sample 50 lemmas (approx. 20%), for a manual inspection. For each lemma, we collected its definitions and the associated year(s) of first attestation from the Sabatini Coletti. Then we manually explored the context of occurrence of each lemma in each time period for each corpus. The manual validation followed a similar approach to the creation of DIACR-Ita gold standard: a lemma is considered to be undergone an LSC only if the definition(s) of the sense are attested in C_2 and not in C_1. The analysis was conducted by only one annotator, who is one of the authors of this paper. By simply using the date of first attestation in the dictionary, 37 lemmas do not qualify as having undergone LSC between the two time periods. Of the remaining 13 lemmas: three have no date of first attestation; five lemmas have a date of first attestation after 1970 (i.e. these lemmas were not used before); and five lemmas present new senses. However, when considering only those lemmas with a new sense attested after 1970, this list reduces to two lemmas.

The manual exploration of the contexts of occurrence in both corpora of the 50 lemmas showed that only four of them (8% of the total sample) can be considered correct examples of an LSC. Two of them, *palmare* ('obvious'/'palmar'/'hand-held computer') and *patteggiare* ('negotiate'/'plea'), are also attested in the Sabatini Coletti. The remaining two, *handicappare* ('to handicap') and *orgasmo* ('orgasm'), indicate a change of use rather than an actual change of meaning. In particular, *handicappare*, and namely its participial form, was used dur-

ing the 80s/90s to refer to people with disabilities, extending the initial meaning in C_1 of "to assign an handicap to a team". The use of the word with this meaning is now derogatory and it is not attested in the dictionary. On the other hand, *orgasmo* was used in C_1 in its figurative meaning of great or extreme anxiety, e.g. "nell'orgasmo del momento" ('in the excitement of the moment'). On the other hand, in C_2 is used with reference to sex and sexuality. Three additional lemmas are signalled as lexical changes: *pula*, *doc*, and *tac*. However, they are officially attested as different lemmas in the Sabatini Coletti, thus implying homonymy. All remaining entries are false positives being either NEs or OCR errors. For the NEs, these are cases where the NE also corresponds to a lemma in the reference dictionary. A good example of this is *borsellino*. In C_1, both corpora present context of use with the dictionary meaning of "a small purse". However, in C_2, the contexts of use refer to the judge Paolo Borsellino[4], killed in a terrorist attack by the Mafia.

NEs introduce additional challenges while constructing a benchmark for LSC, especially when they are homonyms with common nouns. A viable solution to this problem would be to detect and disregard from the corpus those entities that are homonyms of common nouns. This also calls for the development of more robust systems for NE detection: besides our efforts at filtering NEs, lots of them have remained as potential targets of LSC.

---

[4] https://en.wikipedia.org/wiki/Paolo_Borsellino

5 Conclusion and Future Work

This contribution has tested the reliability of the DIACR-Ita benchmark for LSC when the underlying corpus used to train and detect LSCs varies. Furthermore, it has scrutinised the robustness of the LSCs, detected by a common algorithm, across different corpora.

Although preliminary, our results indicate that: (i) social and cultural dimensions must be carefully considered when creating LSC benchmark since potential positive examples may be biased; (ii) current approaches to unsupervised LSC are sensitive to the used corpora; (iii) quality of the data (i.e., OCR rendering) and the presence of NEs, especially homonyms with common nouns, are major sources of errors when such automatic methods are applied to actively discover cases of LSC. Strictly connected to this latter aspect is the hiatus between the results of the algorithm against the benchmark and its use "in the wild". This calls for the development of different and more realistic evaluation protocols for unsupervised LSC and research programmes to address the availability of high quality, distributable diachronic corpora.

Besides these limitations, the use of LSC methods on sources with clear differences along social, political, and cultural dimensions could promote a cross-fertilisation of disciplines.

As future work, we plan to extend our analysis to both other corpora and languages, as well to other lexical change detection algorithms, in order to confirm the validity of our findings.

Acknowledgements

Part of this research was conducted with the financial support of Science Foundation Ireland (Grant Agreement No. 13/RC/2106) at the ADAPT SFI Research Centre at Dublin City University; the EVALITA4ELG project, funded by ELG (European Language Grid) Pilot Projects Open Call 1 (Grant Agreement No. 825627 – H2020, ICT 2018-2020 FSTP). The ADAPT Centre for Digital Media Technology is funded by SFI through the SFI Research Centres Programme and is co-funded under the European Regional Development Fund (ERDF, Grant No. 13/RC/2106_P2).

References

Pierpaolo Basile, Annalina Caputo, Tommaso Caselli, Pierluigi Cassotti, and Rossella Varvara. 2020a. A diachronic italian corpus based on "l'unità". In *Proceedings of the Seventh Italian Conference on Computational Linguistics, CLiC-it 2020, Bologna, Italy, March 1-3, 2021*, volume 2769 of *CEUR Workshop Proceedings*. CEUR-WS.org.

Pierpaolo Basile, Annalina Caputo, Tommaso Caselli, Pierluigi Cassotti, and Rossella Varvara. 2020b. Diacr-ita @ EVALITA2020: overview of the EVALITA2020 diachronic lexical semantics (diacrita) task. In *Proceedings of the Seventh Evaluation Campaign of Natural Language Processing and Speech Tools for Italian. Final Workshop (EVALITA 2020), Online event, December 17th, 2020*, volume 2765 of *CEUR Workshop Proceedings*. CEUR-WS.org.

Stephanie Brandl and David Lassner. 2019. Times are changing: Investigating the pace of language change in diachronic word embeddings. In *Proceedings of the 1st International Workshop on Computational Approaches to Historical Language Change*, pages 146–150, Florence, Italy. Association for Computational Linguistics.

Lea Frermann and Mirella Lapata. 2016. A Bayesian model of diachronic meaning change. *Transactions of the Association for Computational Linguistics*, 4:31–45.

Mario Giulianelli, Marco Del Tredici, and Raquel Fernández. 2020. Analysing lexical semantic change with contextualised word representations. In *Proceedings of the 58th Annual Meeting of the Association for Computational Linguistics*, pages 3960–3973, Online. Association for Computational Linguistics.

Hila Gonen, Ganesh Jawahar, Djamé Seddah, and Yoav Goldberg. 2020. Simple, interpretable and stable method for detecting words with usage change across corpora. In *Proceedings of the 58th Annual Meeting of the Association for Computational Linguistics*, pages 538–555, Online. Association for Computational Linguistics.

Kristina Gulordava and Marco Baroni. 2011. A distributional similarity approach to the detection of semantic change in the Google Books ngram corpus. In *Proceedings of the GEMS 2011 Workshop on GEometrical Models of Natural Language Semantics*, pages 67–71, Edinburgh, UK. Association for Computational Linguistics.

William L Hamilton, Jure Leskovec, and Dan Jurafsky. 2016a. Cultural shift or linguistic drift? comparing two computational measures of semantic change. In *Proceedings of the Conference on Empirical Methods in Natural Language Processing. Conference on Empirical Methods in Natural Language Processing*, volume 2016, page 2116. ACL.

William L Hamilton, Jure Leskovec, and Dan Jurafsky. 2016b. Diachronic Word Embeddings Reveal Statistical Laws of Semantic Change. In *Proceedings* of the 54th Annual Meeting of the Association for Computational Linguistics (Volume 1: Long Papers), pages 1489–1501.

Zellig S Harris. 1954. Distributional structure. *Word*, 10(2-3):146–162.

Simon Hengchen, Nina Tahmasebi, Dominik Schlechtweg, and Haim Dubossarsky. 2021. Challenges for computational lexical semantic change. *arXiv preprint arXiv:2101.07668*.

Jens Kaiser, Dominik Schlechtweg, and Sabine Schulte im Walde. 2020. Op-ims@ diacr-ita: Back to the roots: Sgns+ op+ cd still rocks semantic change detection. *Proceedings of the 7th evaluation campaign of Natural Language Processing and Speech tools for Italian (EVALITA 2020), Online. CEUR. org.*

Yoon Kim, Yi-I Chiu, Kentaro Hanaki, Darshan Hegde, and Slav Petrov. 2014. Temporal analysis of language through neural language models. In *Proceedings of the ACL 2014 Workshop on Language Technologies and Computational Social Science*, pages 61–65, Baltimore, MD, USA. Association for Computational Linguistics.

Rada Mihalcea and Vivi Nastase. 2012. Word epoch disambiguation: Finding how words change over time. In *Proceedings of the 50th Annual Meeting of the Association for Computational Linguistics (Volume 2: Short Papers)*, pages 259–263, Jeju Island, Korea. Association for Computational Linguistics.

Tomas Mikolov, Kai Chen, Greg Corrado, and Jeffrey Dean. 2013. Efficient Estimation of Word Representations in Vector Space. *arXiv preprint arXiv:1301.3781*.

Sunny Mitra, Ritwik Mitra, Martin Riedl, Chris Biemann, Animesh Mukherjee, and Pawan Goyal. 2014. That's sick dude!: Automatic identification of word sense change across different timescales. In *Proceedings of the 52nd Annual Meeting of the Association for Computational Linguistics (Volume 1: Long Papers)*, pages 1020–1029, Baltimore, Maryland. Association for Computational Linguistics.

Matthias Orlikowski, Matthias Hartung, and Philipp Cimiano. 2018. Learning diachronic analogies to analyze concept change. In *Proceedings of the Second Joint SIGHUM Workshop on Computational Linguistics for Cultural Heritage, Social Sciences, Humanities and Literature*, pages 1–11, Santa Fe, New Mexico. Association for Computational Linguistics.

Octavian Popescu and Carlo Strapparava. 2013. Behind the times: Detecting epoch changes using large corpora. In *Proceedings of the Sixth International Joint Conference on Natural Language Processing*, pages 347–355, Nagoya, Japan. Asian Federation of Natural Language Processing.

Dominik Schlechtweg, Barbara McGillivray, Simon Hengchen, Haim Dubossarsky, and Nina Tahmasebi. 2020. SemEval-2020 task 1: Unsupervised lexical semantic change detection. In *Proceedings of the Fourteenth Workshop on Semantic Evaluation*, pages 1–23, Barcelona (online). International Committee for Computational Linguistics.

Dominik Schlechtweg, Sabine Schulte im Walde, and Stefanie Eckmann. 2018. Diachronic usage relatedness (DURel): A framework for the annotation of lexical semantic change. In *Proceedings of the 2018 Conference of the North American Chapter of the Association for Computational Linguistics: Human Language Technologies, Volume 2 (Short Papers)*, pages 169–174, New Orleans, Louisiana. Association for Computational Linguistics.

Ludwig Wittgenstein. 2010. *Philosophical investigations*. John Wiley & Sons.

A OP-SGNS Parameters

Parameter	Value
learning rate	0.025
min. frequency	10
downsampling rate	0.001
training epochs	5
negative sampling	5
context window	5
vector dimension	300

Table 2: OP-SGNS Parameters for the creation of the word embeddings.

The initial learning rate is set to 0.025, with a negative sampling of 5 and a context window size fixed to 5.

B Cosine similarities: Spearman Correlations

Figure 2 shows the plots of the Spearman correlations between the two sets of ranked similarities computed over the two sub-corpora, C_1 and C_2, of "L'Unità" and "La Stampa", respectively. The cosine similarities are binned in bin of size 0.05 in the interval $[0.0, 0.9]$. The background histogram reports the binned cosine similarity distribution for "L'Unità" (Figure (a)) and "La Stampa" (Figure (b)). The foreground red plot shows the corresponding Spearman correlation values when computed against the "La Stampa" (Figure (a)) and "L'Unità" (Figure (b)), respectively.

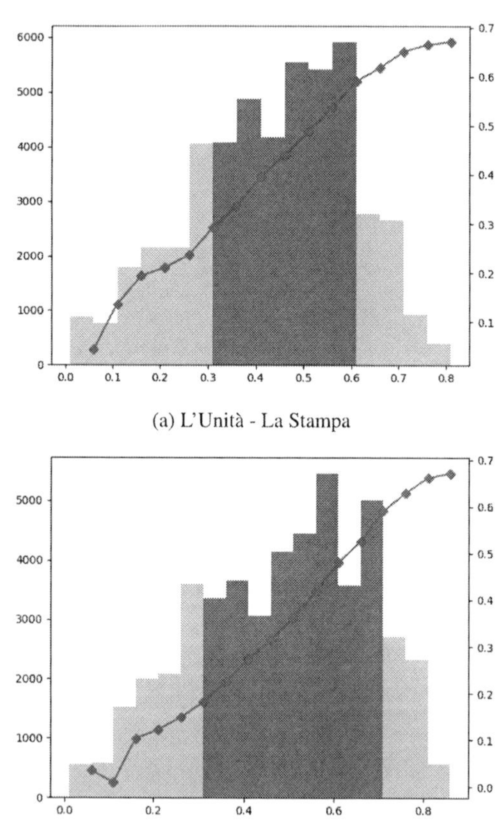

(a) L'Unità - La Stampa

(b) La Stampa - L'Unità

Figure 2: Correlation plots.

Linguistic change and historical periodization of Old Literary Finnish

Niko Partanen, Khalid Alnajjar, Mika Hämäläinen and Jack Rueter
Faculty of Arts
University of Helsinki & Rootroo Ltd
`firstname.lastname@helsinki.fi`

Abstract

In this study, we have normalized and lemmatized an Old Literary Finnish corpus using a lemmatization model trained on texts from Agricola. We analyse the error types that occur and appear in different decades, and use word error rate (WER) and different error types as a proxy for measuring linguistic innovation and change. We show that the proposed approach works, and the errors are connected to accumulating changes and innovations, which also results in a continuous decrease in the accuracy of the model. The described error types also guide further work in improving these models, and document the currently observed issues. We also have trained word embeddings for four centuries of lemmatized Old Literary Finnish, which are available on Zenodo.

1 Intoduction

In this study, we investigate linguistic drift and historical periodization of Old Literary Finnish. We use a historical Finnish lemmatizer model trained on the works of Mikael Agricola, and apply the model to the remaining currently available corpus of Old Literary Finnish (Institute for the Languages of Finland, 2013). This allows us to examine both the differences in the model's performance and how the lexicon of Old Literary Finnish has changed and evolved over time.

We hypothesize that the contexts where the model's quality changes significantly correlate, in fact, with changes in the actual form of the literary language. These can be innovations in the orthography, or other kinds of linguistic changes that are known to have happened during the period Finnish has been a written language. Careful error detection should also reveal something about the nature of these changes. As long as the model's quality remains above a specific threshold, we should also be able to monitor the use of specific lexemes over

time. We trained the word embeddings for this purpose. The corpus size being limited, and divided to time period of 1543–1809, we concluded that more data is needed to follow the actual semantic changes.

2 Related work

Natural language processing for Old Literary Finnish is still in a very early stage, while extensive work already exists for historical variants of other languages (Dubossarsky et al., 2019; Perrone et al., 2019; Hill and Hengchen, 2019; Degaetano-Ortlieb et al., 2021). Most work has been done with historical newspapers, which represent only later periods of this language variety, starting from 1771. Many studies are connected to improving OCR accuracy, which remains as an important task for old printed materials. Recognizing named entities is another line of research that has been developed relatively far, especially by Kettunen and Ruokolainen (2017), Kettunen et al. (2016a) and Kettunen and Löfberg (2017). This connects to other work in NER of other Finnish varieties (Porjazovski et al., 2020; Ushio and Camacho-Collados, 2021).

Also evaluation and post processing approaches are closely connected to our study. Kettunen and Pääkkönen (2016) and Kettunen et al. (2016b) used a morphological analyser adapted for historical Finnish to evaluate OCR accuracy in these newspapers. Later on, OCR accuracy has been improved through unsupervised post-correction in Finnish newspapers (Duong et al., 2020).

Koskenniemi and Kuutti (2017) studied alignment and analysis of Old Literary Finnish, using a Helsinki Finite-State Transducer (Lindén et al., 2013). Lexical change through neologisms has been studied in historical data by comparing word occurrences in a historical corpus to earliest attestations recorded in dictionaries (Säily et al., 2021).

Proceedings of the 2nd International Workshop on Computational Approaches to Historical Language Change 2021, pages 21–27
August 6, 2021. ©2021 Association for Computational Linguistics

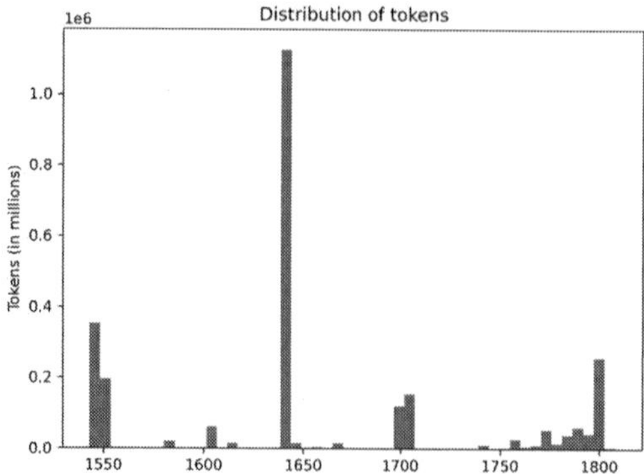

Figure 1: Distribution of tokens in the Corpus of Old Literary Finnish

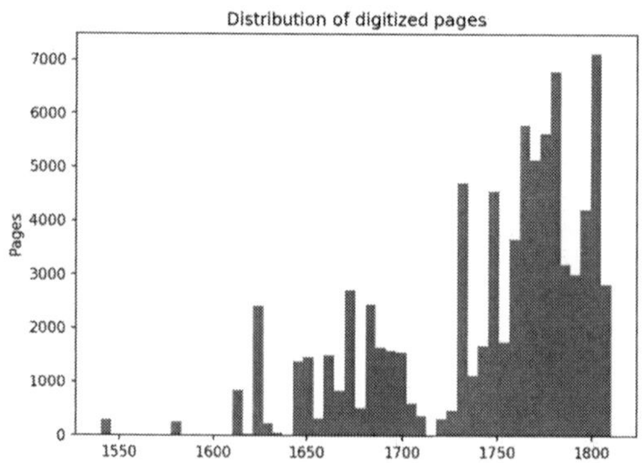

Figure 2: Digitized Finnish pages in the National Library of Finland's Digital collections (May 2021)

3 Data

We use the Old Literary Finnish corpus (Institute for the Languages of Finland, 2013). This is the only proofread corpus of Old Literary Finnish currently available, it aims to be representative, and is created especially for the purposes of lexicography. The current corpus is 4.13 million tokens in size. The distribution of tokens by year is shown in Figure 1. To contextualize the distribution, the Bible translation from year 1642 contains over a million tokens. The corpus has 1.5 million tokens where the year is not defined in the metadata, and thereby were not included in our study.

In order to better understand the relationship this data has to the entire Old Literary Finnish corpus, we can compare it to various adjacent sources. The first logical point of comparison is the national metadata catalogs, which should contain relatively complete information about all books that have ever been printed. This data was already analysed by (Tolonen et al., 2019), and their figures are certainly worth comparing in this context, too.

As text sources, however, these materials are only useful for us if they have been digitized and can be accessed. To understand this context, we examined the number of digitized pages from the same time period in the collections of the National Library of Finland[1]. The distribution of digitized Finnish pages is shown in Figure 2.

This shows that our current sample is still relatively small, and many different sample constellations could be imagined. Comparing to (Tolonen et al., 2019), for example, it seems that the dip in digitized pages we see in Figure 2 in the first half of the 18th century does not seem to correlate with a reduced printing activity in this time period. Similarly the Old Literary Finnish corpus has four larger peaks, representing, presumably, the goal to include all four centuries of this language variety to a comparable degree.

Besides the proofread portion of the corpus, the materials of Agricola have been published as a morphosyntactically annotated version (Institute for the Languages of Finland and University of Turku, 2020). Each resource type we have discussed above is narrower than the one before, as specialized annotation, proofreading and digitization are all resource demanding activities. Our work explores what we can do with the current data, existing annotations, and how we can build NLP solutions around these materials to extend and enrich the available resources. Publishing our word embeddings also contributes to this goal.[2]

For evaluation purposes, we have also created our own manually lemmatized dataset.[3] This ground truth material was created where possible with the Dictionary of Old Literary Finnish (Kotimaisten kielten keskus, 2021). Since the dictionary only currently extends to the word *perstauta* 'to rot; to decay', however, there are instances where we could not consult this resource, and had to decide the evaluated lemma with our own linguistic intuition. For example, one description of metallurgy practices from 1797 contains the segment *jotka makawat palkein ylitze ja wääteillä* 'which lie over the bellows and [unknown word]' [Rin1797-49]. The wordform *wääteillä* is not in the dictionary, and it occurs only in this decade in the currently available corpus. We have lemmatized this lexeme as *vääde*, with full knowledge that this may be erroneous. As our dataset is openly available, the errors are easily corrected later. This illustrates how extremely complicated tasks normalization and lemmatization of historical texts are, and we approach this question with the goal to evaluate the currently available methods, and to improve our understanding on how to improve our models.

4   Experiment design

We used an Old Literary Finnish lemmatizer (Hämäläinen et al., accepted) trained with manually lemmatized corpus form Agricola (Institute for the Languages of Finland and University of Turku, 2020). The lemmatization model reached 96.3% accuracy in texts written by Agricola, and 87.7% accuracy in out-of-domain data (Hämäläinen et al., accepted). The model follows the same LSTM architecture that has been found useful both for modern Finnish normalization (Partanen et al., 2019) and dialectalization (Hämäläinen et al., 2020).

Our hypothesis is that if we evaluate the errors the model makes with the texts originating from different periods, we can use the errors as a proxy for progressing changes. These results can be later verified and dated more accurately with larger corpora as such resources become available.

For our error analysis, we have selected 25 sentences from different decades, and manually lemmatized them. If a decade had a smaller number of sentences, then we took all the sentences available. The manual annotations are used as the gold standard against which the model's predictions are compared. This results in a manually corrected dataset of 476 sentences.

5   Result

We find that the word error rate (WER) of the lemmatization model fluctuates between 1–23% in our test dataset. The WER, however, increases gradually when measured by the decade, and our hypothesis is that this change represents the linguistic distance that increases when new vocabulary and conventions are added to the written standard.

This can be tested through a detailed error classification and analysis, which we conduct in the next section. Whenever possible, we aim to provide estimations of when different features emerge, which hopefully allows to detect various periods that can be distinguished from one another.

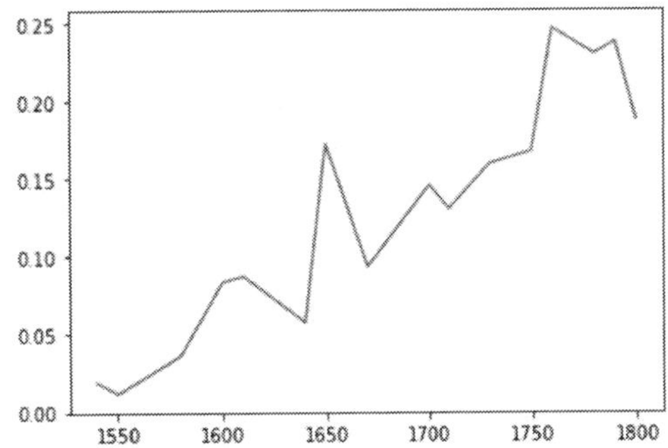

Figure 3: Word Error Rate per decade

6   Error analysis

6.1   Agricola texts

Although the model was trained with the Agricola data, there are still individual errors even in this material. These relate often to personal names such as *Ziphi* and *Zipheis*, which in the original corpus were normalized as *Sifi*. In the vicinity of these words the normalization is very good, and generally we do not find that lemma level errors would impact a more extensive sentence.

We presume these are words which have not occurred in the original training data, where part of the Agricola corpus was used as the test data, or then forms are simply too rare or exceptional. Needless to say, as the Figure 3 shows the accuracy is almost flawless in the earliest portion of the corpus. We can illustrate the accuracy with an example from Agricola's Prayer book. The original sentence is *Mine rucolen sinua sinun poias cautta* 'I pray for you through your son' [rk1544-647]. The correct lemmatization is *minä rukoilla sinä sinä poika kautta*, which is exactly what the model outputs.

6.2   Emerging changes

It appears that the errors are strongly connected to new types of linguistic content and writing conventions. For example, Agricola never used the pronoun form *sä* 'you', opting for full forms instead, as illustrated in example above. Once the shorter form starts to appear, the model is not always able to normalize them correctly. For example, from 1616 there is an example *Sä quin ryövärille jaoid Paradiisin perimisen* 'As if you shared the inheritance of Paradise with the robber' [Hemm1616-50], where the first pronoun is normalized with the verb *säätää* 'to ordain', which is entirely incorrect. The model is clearly extremely sensitive to small differences in the spelling conventions. We can see this well in spelling variants that are used only by individual authors. For example, *neidzö* appears to be used only in texts by Jacobus Petri Finno from 1583 (for example, see [FinnoVk-4:15-3a]). We presume the actual distributions of different variants are larger, just not yet visible in this corpus.

We can also point out that the model leaves numbers untouched, but larger years are usually restructured, so that 1761 becomes 1161. In Agricola's materials there are no larger years than 1551, which is when his Book of Psalms was published.

6.3 Challenge of multilinguality

Another type of errors comes from materials in languages other than Finnish. Currently, these are left out from the accuracy count, but they are present in our balanced sample. These include, for example Latin phrases such as: *Magi de longe veniunt Aurum Thus Myrrham offerunt / Intrantes domum in vicem Natum salutant homines.* [FinnoVk-51:0-46b]. What the model returns is *magi de loki vene auru tus myrha oferu / intrante tuomus ja viedä natus saluttaa huomines.* As we see, it has tried to normalize Latin into Finnish, which obviously fails. In the future it will be important to investigate whether the same model can be used with different languages, or if we can teach the model to ignore non-Finnish content, so that they could be processed with more suitable tools. Another instance like this is the Greek phrase *kyrie eleison* 'Lord, have mercy', which is not used by Agricola.

There are also multiple instances of foreign names that the model cannot process. Names such as *Küttleri*, *Sinclair* and *Gezelius* are not processed correctly. The ideal behaviour for the model would be to leave proper nouns unnormalized, other than lemmatizing them into the nominative singular. Currently the model often returns a close approximation of this, but names such as *Gezelius* are slightly normalized to *geselius*. Similarly *Stockholmin* is lemmatized into *tokkolma*. This is a common problem with many neural models: the number of potential new or foreign proper nouns that can occur in the text is enormous, and they regularly contain characters and character sequences that have not been seen before. However, similar issues are also met with Finnish toponyms such as *Tammela* and *Jokiainen*, so the problems are not exclusively related to foreign names.

6.4 Evolving punctuation & conventions

The use of comma was not yet characteristic for Agricola's materials. Interestingly, in the contemporary handwritten Westh Codex the comma is regularly used. We find increasing use of the comma from 1640, and after 1740 it appears to be fully established alongside other modern punctuation. The change has been gradual, and deserves further investigation. For the periodization the use of modern punctuation would be an obvious candidate, as we could possibly split the material into sections before and after the emergence of this practice. It seem that the process has been gradual. For example, Petraeus in 1656 has already begun using rather modern punctuation, including regular use of the comma. However, not exclusively, and / can also be seen to have a function. 1700 is the last decade when / is regularly used in writing. More comprehensive corpus would certainly allow more nuanced analysis. This is also a decade in which we see a massive increase in the use of hyphens to separate elements in the compounds. Still, the use of the comma is entirely new to the model, and these are regularly returned as numbers or individual letters.

Another distinction that emerges in the 18th century is the use of the section sign, §. Our first occurrence is in an almanac from 1705, after which they become common: especially so in almanacs and legal texts. Thereby this also connects to the differentiation of text genres. In 1640s we see that the accuracy improves in relation to previous decades. Since most of the data from that period comes from a Bible translation, we believe there is a domain match with Agricola's data, which improves the performance.

We can also point out the increased use of abbreviations separated from case marking with a colon, such as the word 'majesty' in *Cosca Kuningallisen Maj:tin uscollinen Mies* 'Because of the man loyal to the his majesty the King' [ZLith1718-1]. Agricola doesn't yet use this convention, so the model has never encountered it, and cannot normalize these instances correctly. In the current corpus this convention is used in other texts but not in Agricola, which makes it impossible to date more exactly when it has started to be used. For the future work, we would suggest to train the model so that abbreviations are expanded automatically.

6.5 Expanding domains & vocabulary

Especially in the newer data we see the domain difference growing. For example, in Frosterus's 1791 work *Hyödyllinen Huwitus Luomisen Töistä* 'Beneficial pastime in the work of creation' among the topics discussed are planets and other modern scientific concepts, which include terminology the model has never seen. Yet, we can see that the model has some internal logic also here. Word *planetit* 'planets (modern spelling *planeetat*)' is lemmatized as *planetti*, which is not the contemporary singular form *planeetta*, but still a reasonable guess from the old spelling. This can be compared to Lissander's 1793 publication *Maa-Pärunain Kasswattamisesta* 'On the growing of potatoes'. Again, the model is not able to handle the entirely new type of terminology, including plants. As this terminology is often borrowed, it is even more difficult to normalize. The task we are performing is also somewhat more challenging than just lemmatization, as we have combined it with the normalization to modern Finnish. Thereby the correct lemma for word *soldati* 'soldier' would be *sotilas*, and not *soltatti* the model currently proposes. Similarly normalizing the word *phasianus* 'Common pheasant' as *fasaani* would probably require information the model currently cannot have. Naturally, it is another question in itself how these words should be lemmatized, and whether the contemporary Finnish should even be used as the desired target.

In a recent study that investigated neural morphological models for different languages one of the found error types were the unknown and foreign words that were phonotactically or orthographically unusual (Hämäläinen et al., 2021). We believe this process is present also here, when neural model fails to generalize to the input that contains innovations that are beyond the patterns in the training data, even though there is some generic capacity to deal with unseen material.

6.6 What about the periodization?

We believe that detecting and delineating different periods when the features emerge and become established is important, as the process how they have spread and become adapted may be very relevant for both historical and linguistic studies. By understand how the material differentiates we can also design our tools in more systematic and appropriate manner. However, as illustrated in Figure 1, the currently used corpus is not temporally perfectly representative, as there are several periods with no data available. Our analysis also suggests that the change is gradual and complex, and very clear cut periods cannot necessarily be found. In this point we refrain from presenting more definite numbers, as those are necessarily connected to conventions in individual works in our small sample, and the wider relationship between the texts cannot be seen.

In order to do periodization successfully more data is needed. However, many of these materials have been digitized (See Figure 2), and are in Public Domain. The path toward such a task is thereby open, and we hope our methodological demonstration in this study also contributes into this work.

7 Conclusion

We show that analysing the errors produced by a neural network that is trained for one task in one specific material serves as a good indicator for salient and emerging differences between the texts. The methodological contribution of our study is that we can use neural networks effectively to track these changes. We could not successfully split the material into distinct periods, but we propose this can be done. Still, we were able to trace the changes in some phenomena, especially the punctuation conventions. We see more of a gradual process than clear phases, which also indicates that our initial goal of periodization may not be ideal.

The most important finding of our study is that the proposed method works. As the error rate of the neural network increases linearly with newer material, we are convinced that this signals the increasing differentiation of the data in these periods when compared to the texts written by Agricola.

Although in reality there is no need to process Old Literary Finnish materials with the data from Agricola alone, besides the fact that only this material is available for training, we think the experiment design also has relevance for NLP research more generally. The language changes also in our day, and the models we train should be able to handle innovations that are only currently emerging. Therefore the test setting, although artificial, asks a question that is worth presenting.

Very importantly, our study provides a clear roadmap for the further development of normalization and lemmatization of Old Literary Finnish. As we published our models and materials openly in Zenodo, our analysis is easy to reproduce, and our initial benchmark can be improved.

References

Stefania Degaetano-Ortlieb, Tanja Säily, and Yuri Bizzoni. 2021. Registerial adaptation vs. innovation across situational contexts: 18th century women in transition. *Frontiers in Artificial Intelligence*, 4:56.

Haim Dubossarsky, Simon Hengchen, Nina Tahmasebi, and Dominik Schlechtweg. 2019. Time-out: Temporal referencing for robust modeling of lexical semantic change. In *Proceedings of the 57th Annual Meeting of the Association for Computational Linguistics*, pages 457–470.

Quan Duong, Mika Hämäläinen, and Simon Hengchen. 2020. An unsupervised method for OCR post-correction and spelling normalisation for Finnish. *arXiv preprint arXiv:2011.03502*.

Mika Hämäläinen, Niko Partanen, Khalid Alnajjar, Jack Rueter, and Thierry Poibeau. 2020. Automatic dialect adaptation in Finnish and its effect on perceived creativity. In *11th International Conference on Computational Creativity (ICCC'20)*. Association for Computational Creativity.

Mika Hämäläinen, Niko Partanen, Jack Rueter, and Khalid Alnajjar. 2021. Neural morphology dataset and models for multiple languages, from the large to the endangered. In *Proceedings of the 23rd Nordic Conference on Computational Linguistics (NoDaLiDa)*, pages 166–177, Reykjavik, Iceland (Online). Linköping University Electronic Press, Sweden.

Mark J Hill and Simon Hengchen. 2019. Quantifying the impact of dirty ocr on historical text analysis: Eighteenth century collections online as a case study. *Digital Scholarship in the Humanities*, 34(4):825–843.

Mika Hämäläinen, Niko Partanen, and Khalid Alnajjar. accepted. Lemmatization of historical old literary Finnish texts in modern orthography. In *Proceedings of Conférence sur le Traitement Automatique des Langues Naturelles (TALN)*.

Institute for the Languages of Finland. 2013. Corpus of Old Literary Finnish. Saatavilla: https://kaino.kotus.fi/korpus/vks/meta/vks_coll_rdf.xml.

Institute for the Languages of Finland and University of Turku. 2020. The Morpho-Syntactic Database of Mikael Agricola's Works version 1.1.

Kimmo Kettunen and Laura Löfberg. 2017. Tagging named entities in 19th century and modern Finnish newspaper material with a Finnish semantic tagger. In *Proceedings of the 21st Nordic Conference on Computational Linguistics*, pages 29–36.

Kimmo Kettunen, Eetu Mäkelä, Juha Kuokkala, Teemu Ruokolainen, Jyrki Niemi, et al. 2016a. Modern tools for old content-in search of named entities in a Finnish OCRed historical newspaper collection 1771-1910. In *LWDA*, pages 124–135.

Kimmo Kettunen and Tuula Pääkkönen. 2016. Measuring lexical quality of a historical Finnish newspaper collection—analysis of garbled OCR data with basic language technology tools and means. In *Proceedings of the Tenth International Conference on Language Resources and Evaluation (LREC'16)*, pages 956–961.

Kimmo Kettunen, Tuula Pääkkönen, and Mika Koistinen. 2016b. Between diachrony and synchrony: Evaluation of lexical quality of a digitized historical Finnish newspaper and journal collection with morphological analyzers. In *Baltic HLT*, pages 122–129.

Kimmo Kettunen and Teemu Ruokolainen. 2017. Names, right or wrong: Named entities in an OCRed historical Finnish newspaper collection. In *Proceedings of the 2nd International Conference on Digital Access to Textual Cultural Heritage*, pages 181–186.

Kimmo Matti Koskenniemi and Pirkko Kuutti. 2017. Indexing old literary Finnish text. *K+ K= 120 Papers dedicated to László Kálmán and András Kornai on the occasion of their 60th birthdays*.

Kotimaisten kielten keskus. 2021. *Vanhan kirjasuomen sanakirja*. Number 38 in Kotimaisten kielten keskuksen verkkojulkaisuja. Päivitettävä julkaisu. Päivitetty 20.5.2021 [viitattu 7.6.2021]. Available https://kaino.kotus.fi/vks/.

Krister Lindén, Erik Axelson, Senka Drobac, Sam Hardwick, Juha Kuokkala, Jyrki Niemi, Tommi A Pirinen, and Miikka Silfverberg. 2013. HFST a system for creating NLP tools. In *International Workshop on Systems and Frameworks for Computational Morphology*, pages 53–71. Springer.

Niko Partanen, Mika Hämäläinen, Khalid Alnajjar, et al. 2019. Dialect text normalization to normative Standard Finnish. In *The Fifth Workshop on Noisy User-generated Text (W-NUT 2019) Proceedings of the Workshop*. The Association for Computational Linguistics.

Valerio Perrone, Marco Palma, Simon Hengchen, Alessandro Vatri, Jim Q Smith, and Barbara McGillivray. 2019. Gasc: Genre-aware semantic change for ancient Greek. In *Proceedings of the 1st International Workshop on Computational Approaches to Historical Language Change*, pages 56–66.

Dejan Porjazovski, Juho Leinonen, and Mikko Kurimo. 2020. Named entity recognition for spoken Finnish. In *Proceedings of the 2nd International Workshop on AI for Smart TV Content Production, Access and Delivery*, AI4TV '20, page 25–29, New York, NY, USA. Association for Computing Machinery.

Tanja Säily, Eetu Mäkelä, and Mika Hämäläinen. 2021. From plenipotentiary to puddingless: Users and uses of new words in early English letters. In Mika Hämäläinen, Niko Partanen, and Khalid Alnajjar, editors, *Multilingual Facilitation*. Rootroo Ltd.

Mikko Tolonen, Leo Lahti, Hege Roivainen, and Jani Marjanen. 2019. A quantitative approach to book-printing in Sweden and Finland, 1640–1828. *Historical methods: a journal of quantitative and interdisciplinary history*, 52(1):57–78.

Asahi Ushio and Jose Camacho-Collados. 2021. T-NER: An all-round Python library for transformer-based named entity recognition. In *Proceedings of the 16th Conference of the European Chapter of the Association for Computational Linguistics: System Demonstrations*, pages 53–62, Online. Association for Computational Linguistics.

A diachronic evaluation of gender asymmetry in euphemism

Anna Kapron-King
Department of Computer Science
University of Toronto
annakk@cs.toronto.edu

Yang Xu
Department of Computer Science
Cognitive Science Program
University of Toronto
yangxu@cs.toronto.edu

Abstract

The use of euphemisms is a known driver of language change. It has been proposed that women use euphemisms more than men. Although there have been several studies investigating gender differences in language, the claim about euphemism usage has not been tested comprehensively through time. If women do use euphemisms more, this could mean that women also lead the formation of new euphemisms and language change over time. Using four large diachronic text corpora of English, we evaluate the claim that women use euphemisms more than men through a quantitative analysis. We assembled a list of 106 euphemism-taboo pairs to analyze their relative use through time by each gender in the corpora. Contrary to the existing belief, our results show that women do not use euphemisms with a higher proportion than men. We repeated the analysis using different subsets of the euphemism-taboo pairs list and found that our result was robust. Our study indicates that in a broad range of settings involving both speech and writing, and with varying degrees of formality, women do not use or form euphemisms more than men.

1 Introduction

What role does gender play in language change and use? This question has long been a matter of discussion among linguists. In Robin Lakoff's influential work on this topic, she proposes many ways in which language spoken by women and about women differs from language used by and about men (Lakoff, 1973, 1977). Lakoff discusses the causes of these differences and what they tell us about women's role in society. The difference we focus on in this study is one she mentions only briefly, namely that women use euphemisms more than men do (Lakoff, 1977, p. 78). Lakoff is not the first to propose this difference. Jespersen (2013,

originally published 1922) also claims that women use euphemisms more often, and discusses this supposed characteristic of women's language at length. Both Lakoff and Jespersen believe that women use euphemisms more out of a desire to speak more tactfully and to avoid directly mentioning "unladylike" topics. For example, Jespersen states that women have often invented euphemisms to avoid mentioning "certain parts of the human body and certain natural functions" (2013, p. 245).

Euphemisms have been considered as an important driver of language change (Burridge, 2012). As a euphemism becomes conventionalized, it may become taboo by its association with a taboo topic, and thus ends up being replaced by a new euphemism. This process has been dubbed the *euphemism treadmill* by Pinker (1994). While Lakoff (1977) considers euphemism use to be a sign of linguistic conservatism, given what we know about the euphemism treadmill it may also be reasonable to associate euphemisms with linguistic innovation. Since women are thought to use euphemisms and invent new euphemisms in order to avoid taboo, a finding that women do in fact use euphemisms more could be an indication that women are leading the euphemism treadmill process.

One may take for granted that women use euphemisms more than men, because this idea has been proposed by two renowned linguistics, and with a few decades between them. However, both Jespersen and Lakoff base this claim primarily on anecdotal evidence. To our knowledge, no one has attempted to quantitatively evaluate whether greater use of euphemisms is characteristic of women's speech. Here we analyze euphemism usage through time by men and women in four large text corpora of English to test this claim. Specifically, we examine whether at a given time point in history, women use euphemisms with a greater proportion in usage frequency than men do.

Proceedings of the 2nd International Workshop on Computational Approaches to Historical Language Change 2021, pages 28–38
August 6, 2021. ©2021 Association for Computational Linguistics

2   Related work

2.1   Defining euphemism

Definitions of euphemism can vary (Casas Gómez, 2009). The Oxford English Dictionary (OED) defines a euphemism as "a less distasteful word or phrase used as a substitute for something harsher or more offensive" (oed, 2020). Euphemisms are a common part of everyday polite speech. For example, we might describe certain bodily functions as "going to the bathroom" or when referring to someone who has just died we might say they have "recently passed". Euphemisms can be used to discuss any taboo topic, without directly naming the taboo. Taboo is culturally and contextually dependent, and as such so is euphemism (Allan and Burridge, 2006; Burridge, 2012).

While there is variation in what different people consider to be a euphemism in different contexts, people can judge words to be euphemistic without needing context, such as when they compile euphemism dictionaries (Burridge, 2012). Allan and Burridge consider these judgements to be made following the "middle class politeness criterion" (MCPC) (Allan and Burridge, 2006, p. 33), which vaguely describes a polite, "middle-class environment" where a euphemism might be preferred over a more offensive expression. This is roughly the context we assume in this study.

Following the OED definition of euphemism, we consider only words and phrases as euphemisms, though a euphemism could conceivably be any length of utterance. We also assume here that a euphemism is an expression that substitutes for a taboo expression, though some scholars argue that there is not always a direct correspondence between a euphemism expression and a taboo (Casas Gómez, 2009).

2.2   Gender and language

Throughout many different cultures and languages, it has been observed that men and women use language differently, and some of these differences have been remarked upon for centuries (Lakoff, 1973; Jespersen, 2013; Eckert and McConnell-Ginet, 2013; Holmes, 1997; Coates, 2015; Labov, 1994). This conversation surrounding gender and language has historically often been framed as a characterization of "women's language" (Jespersen, 2013; Lakoff, 1973). Gender differences have been proposed in a wide range of speech characteristics, including word choice, sentence structure, topic choice, and utterance length (Newman et al., 2008). In particular, Lakoff (1973) also proposed that women's speech is more "polite" than men's, and this has been discussed and studied extensively (Holmes, 1997; Brown, 1980; Newman et al., 2008).

There have been many empirical studies of gender differences in language. Newman and colleagues (2008) used text samples to comprehensively investigate a large number of proposed gender differences in language use. Their results did show evidence for some of these differences, but with small effect sizes. Among some of their findings which supported existing claims were that women use pronouns more than men, that men swear more than women, and that women use polite forms (e.g., "Would you mind...") more than men. Newman et al. (2008) did not investigate gender differences in euphemism use, but since euphemisms are often considered a form of polite speech (Allan and Burridge, 2006; Burridge, 2012), their positive finding that women use polite forms more than men may lend credence to the idea that women use euphemisms more.

More recently, Park and colleagues (2016) studied the differences in topics discussed by men and women on Facebook, and how these topics aligned with the interpersonal dimensions of affiliation and assertiveness. They found that women did not use more indirect language than men, contrary to the stereotype that women are less assertive than men and contrary to some of Lakoff's (1973) claims about women's language. Since euphemisms are a form of indirect speech (Allan and Burridge, 2006; Burridge, 2012), this result could be seen to provide evidence against the claim that women use euphemisms more than men.

2.3   Quantitative approaches to lexical semantic change and euphemism

There has been much interest recently in the field of computational linguistics and natural language processing in applying quantitative methods to historical language change, particularly semantic change (Tahmasebi et al., 2018). Existing work has explored aspects including but not restricted to the automatic detection (Sagi et al., 2011; Cook and Stevenson, 2010; Kulkarni et al., 2015; Schlechtweg et al., 2020), laws (Xu and Kemp, 2015; Hamilton et al., 2016; Dubossarsky et al., 2017), and modeling (Frermann and Lapata, 2016;

Bamler and Mandt, 2017; Giulianelli et al., 2020) of semantic change. Differing from this line of work, our focus here is to understand the formation and use of euphemism as a driver of language change. To our knowledge, the closest quantitative approaches to euphemism sought to automatically detect euphemism for content moderation (Zhu et al., 2021) and to classify phrases as euphemistic or dysphemistic using sentiment analysis (Felt and Riloff, 2020), but there exists no quantitative work on characterizing the role of gender in euphemism in a diachronic setting.

We utilize a set of 106 euphemism-taboo pairs and four large diachronic corpora to test whether women use euphemisms with a higher proportion than men. To verify the robustness of our results, we run the analysis on different subsets of euphemism-taboo pairs to mitigate potential issues with our selection of pairs. Throughout these analyses, we find no evidence that women use euphemisms more than men over time.

In the following, we first describe the quantitative methodology we use to investigate the claim that women use euphemisms more than men, and we then discuss the results.

3 Methodology

We quantify euphemism usage by a proportion measure specifying how frequently a given euphemism is used in natural language out of the sum of usage counts of that euphemism and its corresponding taboo expression. This is how we interpret Lakoff and Jespersen's claim that women use euphemisms more. If they only meant that women use euphemisms more without a higher euphemism proportion, then their claim would be simply that women discuss taboo topics more frequently than men, euphemistically or not, which we do not believe is their intention. Hence, we evaluate whether women use euphemisms more by testing whether they tend to have a higher euphemism proportion.

3.1 Diachronic text corpora

We analyzed four large diachronic text corpora covering different time periods. We required corpora for which the author or speaker's gender could be determined for each data point. We chose to use longitudinal corpora because euphemisms are known to change over time, and can often be short-lived (Burridge, 2012), and as such we might expect the usage of a given euphemism to change over time.

The corpora are: Reddit[1], New York Times Annotated Corpus (NYT)[2], Canadian Parliamentary dataset (Canadian Parl.)[3], and United States Congressional dataset (US Congr.)[4] (Rabinovich et al., 2020; Sandhaus, 2008; Beelen et al., 2017; Gentzkow et al., 2018). A summary of statistics for these corpora is shown in Table 1. These corpora represent a variety of registers; two of the corpora are spoken, three are formal, and one is informal from social media. The NYT, Canadian Parl. and US Congr. likely embody the MCPC context described by Allan and Burridge (2006), which makes them good candidates for analyzing euphemism usage. Reddit is a less controlled context, so it may not qualify for the MCPC, which makes it a good point of comparison for the other three corpora.

We did not analyze more dated historical corpora for a few reasons. It would be very difficult for us to judge what should be considered a euphemism 100 or more years ago. We would also need data with a high enough proportion of women authors such that we would not have data sparsity issues, and we expect more recent datasets to have larger proportions of women. The article in which Lakoff says women use euphemisms more was published in 1977 (Lakoff, 1977), which falls within the time span of our analysis.

The US Congr., Canadian Parl., and NYT corpora have a large gender imbalance, with only a small (but increasing) percentage of data each year having been produced by women. We perform the analysis of the US Congr. and Canadian Parl. data beginning in 1951, because from this year on the number of speeches by women per year exceeds our chosen sample size of 100, as we describe later.

3.2 Euphemism-taboo pairs

In order to analyze the usage of euphemisms compared to taboo expressions on a large scale, we need a data source which pairs euphemism expressions with their equivalent taboos. For example:

- passed away (euphemism) → died (taboo)

- bust (euphemism) → breast (taboo)

---

[1] `https://github.com/ellarabi/gender-i diomatic-language`

[2] Only available with license.

[3] `http://lipad.ca`

[4] `https://data.stanford.edu/congress_t ext`

	Reddit	**NYT**	**Canadian Parliament**	**US Congress**
timespan	2006–2020	1987–2007	1951–2018	1951–2010
mean entries per year	8,138,844	88,365	40,756	138,105
initial % entries by women	28%	9%	0.4%	0.6%
final % entries by women	39%	21%	24%	41%

Table 1: A summary of basic statistics for each corpus used in this study. The Canadian Parliament and US Congress datasets are available for earlier years, but the year 1951 was chosen as their starting point because prior to that year the data for women is too sparse.

While there are many euphemism dictionaries (Neaman and Silver, 1995; Rawson, 1981), and the online OED has a "euphemism" category by which to browse dictionary entries, the entries in these references do not provide direct correspondences between euphemisms and taboo expressions. They also tend to include antiquated, overly specialized, and highly polysemous euphemisms. For example, Neaman and Silver include *a green hornet* as a euphemism for a motorcycle traffic policeman in Toronto, Canada (Neaman and Silver, 1995, p.195). To our knowledge, there is no existing list of euphemisms paired with taboo expressions. Our contribution includes a list of 106 pairs of euphemism expressions and taboo expressions, and we have tried by our best judgment to choose expressions found in North American English that are not overly ambiguous or esoteric. Table 2 shows a subset of the pairs that we analyzed. The complete list is available here:

```
https://github.com/annakin6/euphemism-
gender
```

Some of the pairs come from articles which discuss a perceived societal preference for one phrase over another (Collier, 2010; Hayes-Bautista and Chapa, 1987; Martin, 1991; Nowrasteh, 2017; O'Conner and Kellerman, 2012; Sagi et al., 2015; Silver, 2015; Woelfel, 2019; Yandell, 2015), while others we found in euphemism dictionaries and the OED (Neaman and Silver, 1995; OED; Rawson, 1981). A remaining minority of pairs were determined from our own knowledge of euphemisms. The euphemisms were chosen to represent a variety of topics, such as illness, body parts, and war. Previous work has shown that men and women tend to discuss different topics (Newman et al., 2008; Park et al., 2016), so it was important to choose topics that would not favour only men or only women. The same expression sometimes appears in this list as both a taboo and a euphemism (in different pairs). This is because we have included pairs

that represent different stages of the euphemism treadmill.

3.3 Quantification of euphemism usage proportion

To determine euphemism use by gender, we first divided the data according to the speaker's gender. The Reddit data was already separated into self-reported binary gender categories, but the other three corpora did not explicitly contain this information (except for some rare entries in the US Congr. dataset). To classify gender, we first used the speaker's title (e.g., Mr.) if it was clearly masculine or feminine. If the title could not be used, we relied on the R `gender` package to determine gender from the speaker's first name. This package allows for gender retrieval given a first name and a birth year range. Using this package, we created 40-year bins for every decade from 1930 to 1990, and we considered the birth year of a given author/speaker to between 20 to 40 years before the decade that their article/speech was produced. For example, the gender of a speaker from 1951 would be determined from classification data for the birth years 1890–1930. Any texts for which a binary gender classification could not be determined were discarded. For this reason, 17% of the Canadian Parl. data was discarded, 0.04% of the US Congr. data, and 46% of the NYT data.

After dividing by gender, we selected a random sub-sample of fixed size from each gender (100 speeches for Canadian Parl. and US Congr., 1000 articles/posts for NYT and Reddit), to make up for the gender imbalance. For each euphemism-taboo phrase pair we counted the number of times the euphemism and the taboo expression occur in the sample. For each corpus and each pair, we computed a euphemism usage proportion p for each gender, as shown in Equation 1, where f_y^g is the frequency of the expression in the sample for gender

euphemism	taboo	source
african american	black person	(Martin, 1991)
climate change	global warming	(Sagi et al., 2015)
custodian	janitor	(Rawson, 1981)
developing country	third world country	(Silver, 2015)
handicapped	crippled	(O'Conner and Kellerman, 2012)
homemaker	housewife	(Rawson, 1981)
illegal immigrant	illegal alien	(Nowrasteh, 2017)
income inequality	poverty	–
indigenous	native	(Yandell, 2015)
latino	hispanic	(Hayes-Bautista and Chapa, 1987)
overweight	obese	(Collier, 2010)
same-sex	gay	–
underpriviledged	poor	(Rawson, 1981)
undocumented immigrant	illegal immigrant	(Nowrasteh, 2017)

Table 2: A subset of the lemmatized euphemism-taboo pairs used in this study, with their corresponding sources (or – if no source could be identified).

g and year y.

$$p(\text{euphemism}, \text{taboo}, g, y) = \frac{f_y^g(\text{euphemism})}{f_y^g(\text{euphemism}) + f_y^g(\text{taboo})} \quad (1)$$

To ensure plural, past tense, and other inflected forms of the euphemisms are not overlooked, both the corpora and the euphemism-taboo pairs were lemmatized using the `nltk WordNetLemmatizer` and part of speech tagger. This means that each word is reduced to its base lemma, as informed by its part of speech (POS) tag. For example, the word *women*, when its POS is noun, becomes *woman*, and the word *deprived*, when its POS is adjective, remains *deprived*. Lemmatization was used as it provided a more comprehensive and accurate collection of euphemisms in various forms than a stemmer, which just removes affixes, would. For example, the `PorterStemmer` would return *women* and *depriv*, irrespective of POS.

4 Results

We first analyze for all euphemism-taboo pairs, the number of times they are used by each gender, and for how many of these pairs women have a higher euphemism proportion than men do. We then perform focused analyses on selected subsets of the list of euphemism-taboo pairs. These analyses respectively examine: only pairs where the euphemism or taboo is a multi-word phrase, and only pairs which meet the cut-off threshold for all four corpora (i.e., the conjunction set of euphemism-taboo pairs). We find in all the analyses that women do not use euphemisms more than men.

To consider statistical variation in the analyses, we repeatedly sampled 25 times for each gender at each year for each corpus. To alleviate data sparsity, we placed the counts for the US Congr. and Canadian Parl. in 10-year bins, and placed the data for Reddit and NYT in 2-year bins. We also excluded all pairs which did not meet a certain frequency threshold, to eliminate very sparse, unreliable results. For each euphemism-taboo pair and each corpus, we check that both the euphemism and the taboo appear at least once in 10% or more of the 25 samples. If not, we omit that pair from the results for that corpus. The number of pairs out of the 106 that meet the frequency threshold for Reddit is 32, NYT is 80, Canadian Parl. is 35, and US Congr. is 34.

Using a one-tailed Welch's unequal variances t-test, for each pair we compared the euphemism proportions in all 25 samples between genders. We recorded the fraction of pairs for which women had a significantly higher euphemism proportion than men at $p < 0.05$, and vice versa for men. If women use euphemisms more than men, we would expect this to return a large percent of pairs where woman have a higher euphemism proportion than men, and a smaller percent of pairs for men.

Figure 1 shows the euphemism and taboo expression frequencies by gender over time for the pair *lady* (euphemism) vs. *woman*. The top two rows show binned frequencies, and the third row shows

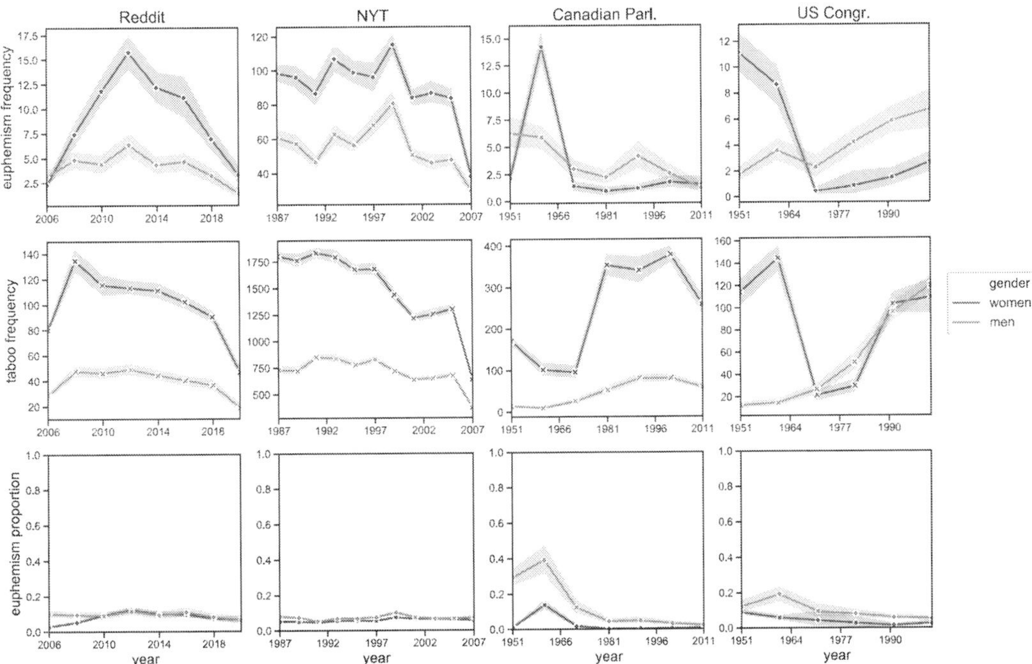

Figure 1: Euphemism and taboo frequencies over time. The top row shows raw euphemism frequency over time, averaged over samples and time spans (span = 2 years for Reddit and NYT, 10 years for Canadian Parl. and US Congr.). The shaded area indicates a 95% confidence interval. The second row shows raw taboo frequency over time, averaged over samples and time spans. The y-axes for the first and second row are not fixed to the same scale, since they are only meant to illustrate the relative difference in frequency for men and women. The third row shows euphemism proportion over time [0,1], as defined in Equation 1. The axis indicating year differs depending on the timescale of the dataset.

the euphemism proportion from Equation 1. This pair is one that specifically relates to women, and that Lakoff (1973) proposed and explained in detail. We see as expected that women say both *lady* and *woman* more than men do. However, women do not say the euphemism *lady* with a higher proportion than men do. In fact, we find that men use this particular euphemism with a substantially higher proportion than women in three of the four corpora for almost their entire time spans.

To summarize the euphemism proportion results, Figure 2 shows the percent of pairs over time where either women have a significantly higher euphemism proportion than men, men have a significantly higher euphemism proportion than women, or neither gender has a significantly higher euphemism proportion.

The individual euphemism-taboo pair plots and the euphemism proportion summary plots show that in all corpora, across the entire time span of 1951–2018, women do not lead in their euphemism-taboo usage proportion. The majority of pairs show no clear leader between men and women. There are some euphemism-taboo pairs where both expressions are said more frequently by women than men, for example women say *lady* and *woman* far more than men do in all four corpora, which is to be expected.

We also repeated this analysis with bins three times larger for each corpus to see if data sparsity affected our results (6 years for Reddit and NYT, 30 years for Canadian Parl. and US Congr.). This increases the number of euphemism-taboo pairs which surpass the frequency threshold for all four corpora, but we found the results still hold that women do not have a consistently higher euphemism proportion than men, and that most pairs show no significant difference in euphemism proportion.

Although we tried not to include many am-

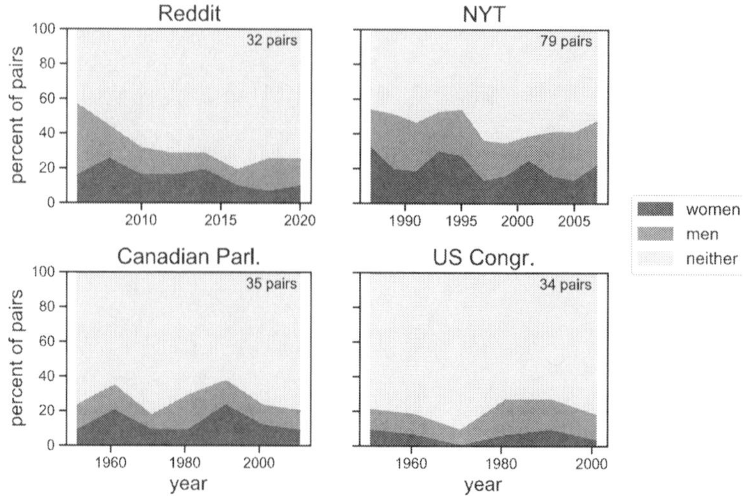

Figure 2: Percentage share of pairs (out of all pairs that met the frequency threshold for a given corpus) for which women have a significantly higher euphemism proportion of usage frequency than men, men have a significantly higher euphemism proportion than women, or neither gender has a significantly higher euphemism proportion.

biguous expressions, some of the words in our euphemism-taboo pair list do contain multiple senses. For example, *weed* could be euphemism for *marijuana* or it could refer to an unwanted plant in a garden. Since multi-word phrases are less likely to have multiple senses, we ran the same analysis on only those euphemism-taboo pairs which contain a multi-word phrase. For example, the pair *armed conflict* and *war*. This analysis does not completely handle ambiguity, since multi-word phrases can be ambiguous and we still permit one of the expressions in the pair to be a single word, however it does help mitigate the effect of expressions with alternative non-euphemistic and non-taboo senses on our results. The results, shown in Figure 3, generally support our finding from the complete analysis that there is a minimal difference in how much men and women use euphemisms. The Reddit and Canadian Parliament graphs show women using euphemisms more, but due to the small sample size (10 pairs and 15 pairs respectively) this result is not very reliable.

For the final analysis, we examine only the pairs which pass the sparsity frequency threshold for every corpus. There are 15 such euphemism-taboo pairs used in this analysis, the results for which are shown in Figure 4. We can also visualize the amount of time for which each gender exhibits a significantly higher euphemism proportion for each pair as a heatmap, shown in Figure 5. The heatmap shows that there are no pairs for which women

consistently have a higher euphemism proportion than men for a larger period of time across all four corpora. However, there are some pairs in some corpora that stick out. The large percent of time for which women have a higher proportion of saying *weed* compared to *marijuana* than men do in the NYT dataset could likely be explained by the fact that *weed* is one of the more ambiguous words in our set of 106 pairs and may be more commonly associated with gardening than marijuana.

These results again support our finding that women do not use euphemisms more than men. There are not many pairs where women have a higher euphemism proportion for very long, and the pairs for which they do are not consistent across corpora. There are, however, a few pairs where men consistently have a higher euphemism proportion than women. For the pair *lady-woman* and the two pairs containing *breast*, men prefer to use the euphemism more than women do, across all four corpora.

5   Discussion

Our analysis of four large, varied datasets spanning 1951–2018 provides no support for Lakoff and Jespersen's claim that women use euphemisms more than men do. This result means that we cannot assume that women use euphemisms more. In general, we should not take for granted the characterization of women's language that has been proposed by linguists such as Jespersen and Lakoff,

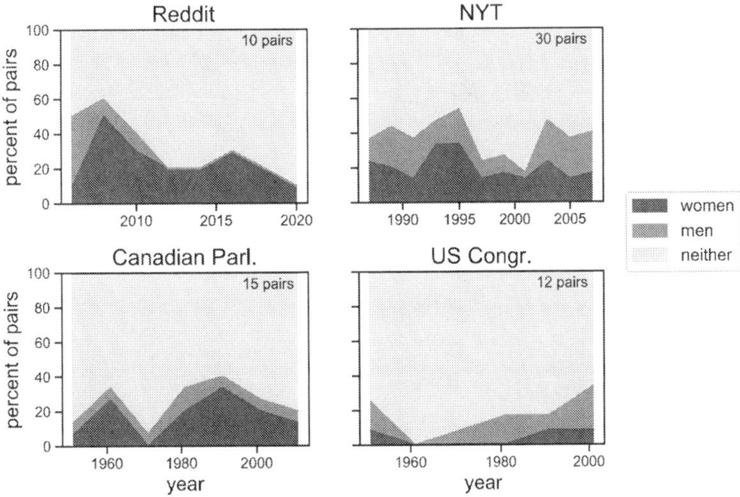

Figure 3: Percent of significant euphemism proportion in the phrase-based analysis. Same as Figure 2 but considering only the euphemism-taboo pairs where at least one of the two expressions is a multi-word phrase.

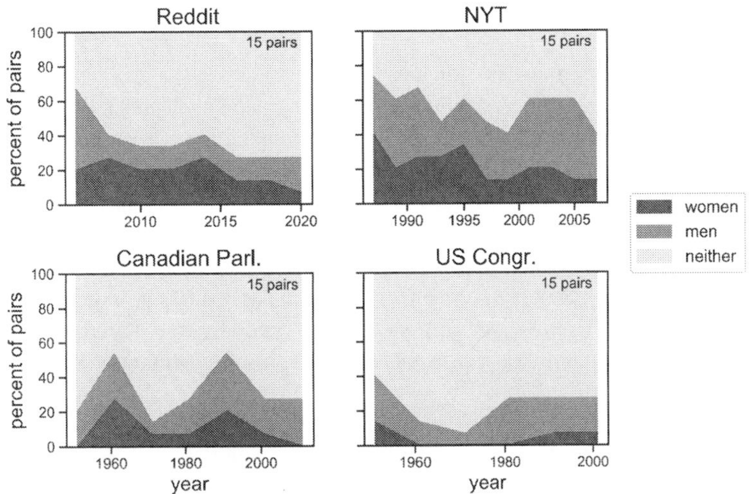

Figure 4: Percent of significant euphemism proportion in the conjunctive pairs. Same as Figure 2 but considering only the euphemism-taboo pairs which meet the threshold for all of the four corpora.

as our study and others have shown that they are not always supported by empirical evidence (Newman et al., 2008; Park et al., 2016).

The result that women do not use euphemisms more indicates that euphemisms should not be lumped in with other polite forms that women were found to use more in other studies (Newman et al., 2008). Our result is consistent with Park et al.'s (2016) finding that women do not tend to use more indirect language than men.

Our finding raises the question, why do Jespersen and Lakoff say that women use euphemisms more if this is not actually the case? One reason women might appear to use euphemisms more is that they may also talk more about certain taboo topics. For example, in our results women say both *chest* and *breast* more than men do, but men say *chest* with a higher proportion than women. The topic of the euphemism seems to have some effect on whether men or women use it more, though at a glance these do not seem to correspond to topics that have been found to be discussed more by one gender or the other. There are of course euphemisms that women do prefer to use more than

pair	women				men			
	Reddit	NYT	Canadian Parl.	US Congr.	Reddit	NYT	Canadian Parl.	US Congr.
('weed', 'marijuana')	0.12	0.82			0.12		0.14	
('sexual assault', 'rape')	0.12	0.091	0.14			0.27		
('pass away', 'die')	0.75	0.27			0.12	0.091	0.29	0.17
('mentally ill', 'insane')	0.38	0.27	0.14			0.18		0.17
('mental illness', 'insanity')	0.38	0.55	0.14	0.17				0.17
('lady', 'woman')					0.25	0.91	1	1
('invalid', 'cripple')	0.12	0.82					0.29	0.33
('insane', 'crazy')	0.12	0.18		0.17		0.091	0.14	
('inner city', 'ghetto')		0.091		0.17			0.14	
('indigenous', 'native')		0.091	0.29		0.12	0.27	0.29	
('fatality', 'death')			0.14		0.12	0.36		0.17
('disabled', 'handicapped')	0.5		0.29			0.64		
('climate change', 'global warming')	0.25	0.091	0.14		0.12	0.27		
('chest', 'breast')				0.17	0.88	1	0.43	0.5
('bust', 'breast')			0.14		1	1	0.57	0.33

Figure 5: Percent of time with significantly higher euphemism proportion (using the same bins we have used throughout, as described in Section 4). The left heatmap indicates for a given (euphemism, taboo) pair for what percent of time women had a significantly higher euphemism proportion for that pair than men did. Darker purple blocks were higher for more time, empty blocks never had a significantly higher euphemism proportion for women. The right heatmap shows the same for men, with darker orange indicating a larger percent of time.

men do, at least within a certain context, such as women on Reddit preferring to say *pass away* over *die* more than men. The claims made by Jespersen and Lakoff could be due to generalizing from specific cases similar to this one. It is also likely that gender differences in language have changed since Jespersen's time – we were unable to investigate this due to data sparsity and a lack of sources for euphemisms from the 1920s. Even so, our corpora spanned 1951–2020 and our finding was consistent throughout that time period.

The four corpora used in this study were chosen because we needed large diachronic corpora for which the author's gender could be approximately determined. However, there are limitations to using these corpora. The language used in political proceedings and in newspapers may be regulated by political parties or the newspaper editors, which might minimize gender differences in language in these corpora. The Reddit data only included posts where users had self-reported gender, which may limit the topics that are included. We did not include any natural conversation data, although that is likely the setting that Lakoff and Jespersen were most concerned with.

There are also limitations to our selected list of euphemism-taboo pairs. The list is relatively small, and was gathered manually. This list does not represent all taboo topics, nor all types of euphemisms. However, we believe it serves as a good first step for quantitative studies of euphemism. Future work on automatic euphemism detection may allow us to generate a more comprehensive list which should help with analyzing euphemism use over time and other related phenomena.

Our study did not directly examine whether women lead euphemism innovation and change, although our result does indicate that this is not likely to be generally true. Future work could investigate who leads the formation of new euphemisms and who drives the euphemism treadmill, while considering that the answer to this question is likely context- and topic-dependant.

6 Conclusion

The subject of how women's language and men's language differ is one that has been extensively discussed, and one alleged difference is that women use euphemisms more than men do. However, this claim has been based on anecdotal evidence. Our diachronic evaluation using large corpora spanning multiple decades from a variety of contexts shows that women do not use euphemisms more than men do. Our work indicates the importance of using quantitative methods to evaluate long-held beliefs about language use and language change.

References

2020. euphemism, n. In *OED Online*. Oxford University Press.

Keith Allan and Kate Burridge. 2006. *Forbidden words: Taboo and the censoring of language*. Cambridge University Press.

Robert Bamler and Stephan Mandt. 2017. Dynamic word embeddings. In *Proceedings of the 34th International Conference on Machine learning*.

Kaspar Beelen, Timothy Alberdingk Thijm, Christopher Cochrane, Kees Halvemaan, Graeme Hirst, Michael Kimmins, Sander Lijbrink, Maarten Marx, Nona Naderi, Ludovic Rheault, Roman Polyanovsky, and Tanya Whyte. 2017. Digitization of the Canadian parliamentary debates. *Canadian Journal of Political Science*, 50(3):849–864.

Penelope Brown. 1980. *How and why women are more polite: Some evidence from a Mayan community*. Preager Publishers.

Kate Burridge. 2012. Euphemism and language change: The sixth and seventh ages. *Lexis – Journal in English Lexicology*, (7).

Miguel Casas Gómez. 2009. Towards a new approach to the linguistic definition of euphemism. *Language Sciences*, 31(6):725–739.

Jennifer Coates. 2015. *Women, men and language: A sociolinguistic account of gender differences in language*, 3 edition. Routledge.

Roger Collier. 2010. Who you calling obese, Doc? *Canadian Medical Association Journal*, 182(11):1161–1162.

Paul Cook and Suzanne Stevenson. 2010. Automatically identifying changes in the semantic orientation of words. In *Proceedings of the 7th International Conference on Language Resources and Evaluation*.

Haim Dubossarsky, Daphna Weinshall, and Eitan Grossman. 2017. Outta control: Laws of semantic change and inherent biases in word representation models. In *Proceedings of the 2017 Conference on Empirical Methods in Natural Language Processing*, pages 1136–1145.

Penelope Eckert and Sally McConnell-Ginet. 2013. *Language and gender*, 2 edition. Cambridge University Press.

Christian Felt and Ellen Riloff. 2020. Recognizing euphemisms and dysphemisms using sentiment analysis. In *Proceedings of the Second Workshop on Figurative Language Processing*, pages 136–145, Online. Association for Computational Linguistics.

Lea Frermann and Mirella Lapata. 2016. A bayesian model of diachronic meaning change. *Transactions of the Association for Computational Linguistics*, 4:31–45.

Matthew Gentzkow, Jesse M. Shapiro, and Matt Taddy. 2018. Congressional record for the 43rd-114th Congresses: Parsed speeches and phrase counts.

Mario Giulianelli, Marco Del Tredici, and Raquel Fernández. 2020. Analysing lexical semantic change with contextualised word representations. In *Proceedings of the 58th Annual Meeting of the Association for Computational Linguistics*, pages 3960–3973, Online. Association for Computational Linguistics.

William L. Hamilton, Jure Leskovec, and Dan Jurafsky. 2016. Diachronic word embeddings reveal statistical laws of semantic change. In *Proceedings of the 54th Annual Meeting of the Association for Computational Linguistics (Volume 1: Long Papers)*, pages 1489–1501, Berlin, Germany. Association for Computational Linguistics.

David E. Hayes-Bautista and Jorge Chapa. 1987. Latino terminology: Conceptual bases for standardized terminology. *American Journal of Public Health*, 77(1):61–68.

Janet Holmes. 1997. Women, language and identity. *Journal of Sociolinguistics*, 1(2):195–223.

Otto Jespersen. 2013. *Language: Its nature and development*, chapter 13. Routledge. Original work published 1922.

Vivek Kulkarni, Rami Al-Rfou, Bryan Perozzi, and Steven Skiena. 2015. Statistically significant detection of linguistic change. In *Proceedings of the 24th International Conference on World Wide Web*.

William Labov. 1994. *Principles of linguistic change*, volume 2 of *Language in Society*. Blackwell.

Robin Lakoff. 1973. Language and woman's place. *Language in Society*, 2(1):45–80.

Robin Lakoff. 1977. You say what you are: Acceptability and gender-related language. In Sidney Greenbaum, editor, *Acceptability in Language*. De Gruyter Mouton.

Ben L. Martin. 1991. From Negro to Black to African American: The power of names and naming. *Political Science Quarterly*, 106(1):83–107.

Judith S. Neaman and Carole G. Silver. 1995. *The Wordsworth book of euphemism*, 2 edition. Wordsworth.

Matthew L. Newman, Carla J. Groom, Lori D. Handelman, and James W. Pennebaker. 2008. Gender differences in language use: An analysis of 14,000 text samples. *Discourse Processes*, 45(3):211–236.

Alex Nowrasteh. 2017. The use of euphemisms in political debate. *Cato Institute*. `https://www.cato.org/blog/use-euphemisms-political-debate`.

Patricia T. O'Conner and Stewart Kellerman. 2012. Crippled, handicapped, disabled? *Grammarphobia*. https://www.grammarphobia.com/blog/201 2/07/crippled-handicapped-disabled.htm l.

OED. 1989. OED Online. http://www.oed.com/. Accessed: 2020-04-06.

Gregory Park, David Bryce Yaden, H. Andrew Schwartz, Margaret L. Kern, Johannes C. Eichstaedt, Michael Kosinski, David Stillwell, Lyle H. Ungar, and Martin E. P. Seligman. 2016. Women are warmer but no less assertive than men: Gender and language on Facebook. *PLOS ONE*, 11(5):e0155885.

Steven Pinker. 1994. The game of the name. *The New York Times*.

Ella Rabinovich, Hila Gonen, and Suzanne Stevenson. 2020. Pick a fight or bite your tongue: Investigation of gender differences in idiomatic language usage. In *Proceedings of the 28th International Conference on Computational Linguistics*.

Hugh Rawson. 1981. *A dictionary of euphemisms & other doubletalk*, 1 edition. Crown Publishers, Inc.

Eyal Sagi, Timothy M. Gann, and Teenie Matlock. 2015. The moral rhetoric of climate change. In *Proceedings of the 37th Annual Conference of the Cognitive Science Society*, page 2063–2068.

Eyal Sagi, Stefan Kaufmann, and Brady Clark. 2011. Tracing semantic change with latent semantic analysis. *Current methods in historical semantics*, 73:161–183.

Evan Sandhaus. 2008. The New York Times annotated corpus.

Dominik Schlechtweg, Barbara McGillivray, Simon Hengchen, Haim Dubossarsky, and Nina Tahmasebi. 2020. Semeval-2020 task 1: Unsupervised lexical semantic change detection. *arXiv preprint arXiv:2007.11464*.

Mark Silver. 2015. If you shouldn't call it the Third World, what should you call it? *NPR.org*. https://www.npr.org/sections/goatsandsoda/20 15/01/04/372684438/if-you-shouldnt-cal l-it-the-third-world-what-should-you -call-it.

Nina Tahmasebi, Lars Borin, and Adam Jatowt. 2018. Survey of computational approaches to lexical semantic change. *arXiv preprint arXiv:1811.06278*.

Mariah Woelfel. 2019. Pot? weed? marijuana? what should we call it? *WBEZ*. https://www.npr.or g/local/309/2019/09/19/762044859/pot-w eed-marijuana-what-should-we-call-it.

Yang Xu and Charles Kemp. 2015. A computational evaluation of two laws of semantic change. In *Proceedings of the 37th Annual Meeting of the Cognitive Science Society*.

Kay Yandell. 2015. Indian, Native, Indigene: The reverberations of a quiet linguistic revolution. *American Literary History*, 27(2):374–391.

Wanzheng Zhu, Hongyu Gong, Rohan Bansal, Zachary Weinberg, Nicolas Christin, Giulia Fanti, and Suma Bhat. 2021. Self-supervised euphemism detection and identification for content moderation. *arXiv preprint arXiv:2103.16808*.

The GLAUx corpus: methodological issues in designing
a long-term, diverse, multilayered corpus of Ancient Greek

Alek Keersmaekers
KU Leuven
alek.keersmaekers@kuleuven.be

Abstract

This paper describes the GLAUx project ("the Greek Language Automated"), an ongoing effort to develop a large long-term diachronic corpus of Greek, covering sixteen centuries of literary and non-literary material annotated with NLP methods. After providing an overview of related corpus projects and discussing the general architecture of the corpus, it zooms in on a number of larger methodological issues in the design of historical corpora. These include the encoding of textual variants, handling extralinguistic variation and annotating linguistic ambiguity. Finally, the long- and short-term perspectives of this project are discussed.

1 Introduction

The increasing availability of large-scale corpus resources has had a lasting impact on the field of linguistics. In the field of corpus linguistics, large quantities of data have made it possible to precisely model complex multifactorial processes of linguistic change (e.g. Perek and Hilpert, 2017; Gries et al., 2018). Modern methods in natural language processing also increasingly make use of word embeddings, which encode rich information about the use of a word learned from large datasets (Collobert et al., 2011; see Kutuzov et al., 2018 for diachronic word embeddings).

From a diachronic perspective, the Greek language corpus is an ideal candidate for a large-scale corpus-linguistic approach: it is not only one of the longest preserved languages (with a large body of text already in the 8th century BC, and continuing up until the present day), but it also is extremely well-documented: the *Thesaurus Linguae Graecae* library of Ancient Greek literary texts, for example, contains more than 110 million words (Pantelia, 2021). To make such an approach possible, this paper will describe *GLAUx* ("the

Greek Language Automated"), a project aiming to collect a large corpus (spanning sixteen centuries) of Ancient Greek texts from various sources and to automatically annotate this corpus for rich linguistic information.

The construction of such a long-term historical corpus is obviously not a trivial task. The goal of this paper is therefore to describe the central problems encountered during this endeavor and the approaches currently adopted to tackle these problems. This will be discussed in section 3, after giving an overview of the data and annotation layers in section 2. Finally, section 4 will give an outlook of future work for this (long-term) project.

2 The corpus

2.1 Text types

Greek texts are usually classified into three categories: literary, papyrological and epigraphical texts. 'Literary' texts are typically transmitted to us through the manuscript tradition. Papyrological and epigraphical texts are written on soft materials such as papyrus and hard materials such as stone respectively, and preserved in their original state. This material dimension also correlates with a genre dimension: 'literary' texts were considered important enough by medieval monks to be copied, and include a wide range of texts (usually, but not always, in a high register), i.e. not only creative text genres such as poems and narrative prose, but also e.g. scientific texts, oratory, philosophical and religious texts. 'Papyrological' and 'epigraphical' texts include all sorts of everyday writing, including letters, receipts and petitions (typically written on papyrus) or texts that are meant to be

Proceedings of the 2nd International Workshop on Computational Approaches to Historical Language Change 2021, pages 39–50
August 6, 2021. ©2021 Association for Computational Linguistics

more durable, e.g. decrees, epitaphs and honorary inscriptions (typically written on stone).[1]

2.2 Related work

Corpus work for Greek started with the development of the *Thesaurus Linguae Graecae* (TLG) in 1972, a full text library of literary texts, currently spanning the 8th century BC to the 15th century AD (Pantelia, 2021). While this project undoubtedly contains the largest collection of Greek text to date (more than 110 million words), and also includes high-accuracy lemmatization, its texts are not publicly available but can only be accessed through a search engine, heavily restricting any possibilities for serious corpus linguistic research as a consequence. An open source alternative is the *Perseus Digital Library* (Crane, 2021) and the *First One Thousand Years of Greek* project (First1K; Crane et al., 2021), both now included in the international *Open Greek and Latin* project. In comparison with the *TLG*, however, their coverage is more restricted (in total about 31 million Greek words, and most texts are situated before the 4th century AD) and the texts are often based on older editions. Non-literary Greek texts are made available by the *Packard Humanities Institute* [2] (epigraphy; see Iversen, 2007) and the Integrating Digital Papyrology project (papyri; Cayless et al., 2021).

While the projects mentioned above only include the full text, there have also been some efforts to add linguistic annotation. A wide variety of treebanking projects have manually annotated Greek texts for morphology, lemmas, (dependency) syntax and sometimes semantics, most prominently the *PROIEL* project (Haug and Johndal, 2008; 277,000 tokens), the *Ancient Greek Dependency Treebanks* (AGDT; Bamman et al., 2009; 560,000 tokens), the *Gorman* trees (Gorman, 2020; 324,000 tokens) and the *Pedalion* project (Keersmaekers et al., 2019; 320,000 tokens), as well as some smaller projects (in total, the manually annotated work includes about 1.5 million tokens). The former two projects are also included in the *Universal Dependencies* (UD) project (Nivre et al., 2016).

There have also been some efforts to annotate even larger amounts of data automatically. Celano (2017) lemmatized and tagged the data of *Perseus* and *First1K* with *Mate* tagger (Bohnet and Nivre, 2012), achieving an accuracy of 88%. The *Diorisis* corpus (Vatri and McGillivray, 2018), including texts from the *Perseus* project and some online sources (about 10 million tokens), was lemmatized and tagged with *TreeTagger* (Schmid 1994), with an accuracy of 91%. There have also been attempts to automatically analyze the papyrus corpus: Celano (2018) achieved a tagging accuracy of 62% and a lemmatization accuracy of 47%, while Keersmaekers (2020b) achieved a morphological tagging accuracy of 95%, 99% for lemmatization, 85% for syntactic parsing and 81% for semantic role labeling. All these automatically analyzed datasets are openly available online.

2.3 Source texts

The source texts for the papyrological part of *GLAUx* and the (planned) epigraphical part are both collected in a single repository (see the previous section). The literary texts, in contrast, are more scattered: while the *TLG* has the most exhaustive collection, its source materials are not publicly available. A large part of the literary corpus has been made available by the *Open Greek and Latin* project (see the previous section), while additional texts can be found on a number of web sources[3] (e.g.). Table 1 gives an overview of the source texts included in the *GLAUx* corpus.

	Tokens	Source
Literary	23.2 million; more to be added	*Open Greek and Latin*; Web
Papyrological	4.5 million	*Integrating Digital Papyrology*
Epigraphical	3.2 million (to be added)	*Packard Humanities Institute*

Table 1: Text types of the *GLAUx* corpus.

---

[1] To refer to texts written on papyrus but that thematically fit better in the literary corpus, the term 'literary papyri' is typically used (while the everyday texts in the papyrus corpus are often called 'documentary papyri'). This paper will use the terms 'literary', 'papyrological' and 'epigraphical' as a genre indicator, i.e. all 'literary' texts, whether transmitted through the manuscript tradition or written on papyrus are called 'literary', while the term 'papyri' is reserved for the documentary papyri.

[2] https://inscriptions.packhum.org

[3] E.g. https://el.wikisource.org; https://www.hs-augsburg.de /~harsch/augustana.html; https://penelope.uchicago.edu /Thayer/E/Roman/Texts/home.html.

In terms of chronology, almost all texts of the papyrological corpus are from the third century BC to the eighth century AD (this is related to the Greek rule of Egypt, where most papyri are found). The epigraphical corpus can generally be dated from the fourteenth century BC to the seventh century AD. The boundaries of the literary corpus are more difficult to define: while it starts with the Homeric poems in the eighth century BC, an end date is more difficult to settle on, as Greek was still widely used until the fall of the Byzantine empire – and continued to be used afterwards (obviously, Greek is still a living language). For the *GLAUx* corpus, we set its boundaries at the eighth century BC to the eighth century AD, so that literary and non-literary texts would be attested in the whole period, while it still contains sixteen centuries of Greek.[4] At the moment of writing, a first version of the full papyrological data as well as an experimental version of the literary data up to the second century AD has been released on GitHub;[5] since the epigraphical corpus has some unique challenges (in particular the high degree of dialectal variation and the lack of epigraphical training data: see 3.1 and 3.2), we plan to add it to *GLAUx* in the long term (see also Dell'Oro and Celano, 2019 for a discussion of some specific issues involved with these texts).

The literary texts have a wide range of text genres, including poetic texts (epic poetry, lyric poetry, tragedy and comedy), philosophic and scientific prose (e.g. medicine, mathematics, geography), historical texts, rhetorical texts, commentaries, religious texts, biographies, narrative fiction, and various other smaller genres. *GLAUx* generally follows the genre classification of the *TLG* in a simplified format (i.e. I assigned just one genre to each text, instead of multiple genres as is sometimes the case with the *TLG* texts), although this classification will be revised in the future to maximize its usefulness for automated processing purposes (see 3.2) and its interoperability with other resources (e.g. the genre classification of the *Diorisis* corpus).[6] For the papyri, the *GLAUx* corpus follows the classification of the *Trismegistos* project (Depauw

and Gheldof, 2014), developed by Joanna Stolk, which includes letters, petitions, contracts, lists, receipts, labels, pronouncements, declarations, reports, accounts, other administrative texts, judicial texts and paraliterary texts as the main text genres.

2.4 Annotation

Due to the size of the *GLAUx* corpus (currently more than 27 million tokens), all annotation was necessarily carried out automatically, building on methods developed by Keersmaekers (2020b) for the papyrus corpus. The treebank data discussed in section 2 was used as training data, which include a wide range of periods and text genres (although most of the data is literary).

Part-of-speech and morphology: For morphological and part-of-speech tagging *RFTagger* was used (Schmid and Laws, 2008), a HMM-based tagger using decision trees to estimate contextual probabilities (as well as suffix features to decide on the lexical probabilities of unknown words). Its output can be constrained by a lexicon that provides possible morphological analyses for each word form, in which case only the morphological analyses present in the lexicon are considered as possible part-of-speech/morphological tags – for this a morphological lexicon generated by the rule-based *Morpheus* morphological analysis tool (Crane, 1991) was used. Prediction accuracy (for the full tag combining part-of-speech and morphological information) ranged from 0.908 (philosophical treatises) to 0.961 (biblical texts), with an average prediction accuracy of 0.945. In terms of text genre, orations, papyri and epic poems also have high accuracy rates, next to biblical texts, while, next to philosophical treatises, comedies, lyric poems and tragedies also have a low accuracy rate (see Table 2).

The morphological annotation is consistent with the (2.0 version) tag set of the *AGDT* (see 2.2). The morphological categories are person, number, tense/aspect, mood, voice, gender, case and degree. Of these, gender, case, tense and mood have the

---

[4] In terms of important linguistic developments, this data includes the Archaic period (8th-6th century BC), which mainly encompasses poetic texts written in a variety of dialects; the Classical period (5th-4th century BC), in which the Attic dialect spoken in Athens became the prestige language of literary texts; the Koine period (3rd century BC-4th century AD), in which Greek became a standardized language since the conquests of Alexander the Great; and the early Medieval period (from the 5th century AD onwards), when Greek was mainly used in the Byzantine empire.

[5] https://github.com/perseids-publications/glaux-trees

[6] See https://perseids-publications.github.io/glaux-trees/ for the current *GLAUx* texts classified by genre.

	Accuracy (N)
Biblical	0.961 (33,994)
Military	0.959 (3,234)
Oratory	0.952 (22,699)
Papyri	0.951 (8,166)
Epic Poetry	0.951 (49,694)
Biography	0.948 (12,265)
History	0.946 (81,560)
Philosophical Dialogue	0.944 (4,146)
Dialogue	0.943 (1,132)
Epistolography	0.941 (1,261)
Narrative Fiction	0.939 (9,883)
Rhetoric	0.937 (3,768)
Polyhistory	0.929 (9,154)
Tragedy	0.924 (21,421)
Lyric Poetry	0.921 (1,084)
Comedy	0.920 (5,640)
Philosophical Treatise	0.908 (9,239)

Table 2: Tagging accuracy by genre.

	Accuracy (N)
Degree	0.995 (49,374)
Number	0.990 (164,492)
Voice	0.987 (48,913)
Part-of-speech	0.985 (278,344)
Person	0.977 (27,728)
Mood	0.970 (27,728)
Tense	0.968 (48,913)
Case	0.959 (136,764)
Gender	0.958 (136,764)

Table 3: Tagging accuracy by morphological attribute.

lowest prediction accuracy (see Table 3), since they include many ambiguous forms (in particular between neuter and masculine, between nominative and accusative and between indicative and subjunctive). Part-of-speech classes are divided into the traditional classes of nouns, adjectives, verbs, adverbs, pronouns, conjunctions, prepositions, numerals, articles and interjections. Since Greek makes a morphological distinction between verbs, nouns, adjectives and uninflected

words, these categories are also relatively easy to handle for the tagger (with a 0.985 accuracy for part-of-speech only).

Currently I am also expanding the morphological annotation with a derivational annotation layer, linking complex morphological derivations (e.g. παιδίον paidíon "little child") to a stem or root (e.g. παιδ- *paid-*, used in the word παῖς *pais* "child") and morphological pattern (e.g. *-ion* diminutives), which will further expand linguistic research possibilities for end users: see Litta et al. (2019) for comparable work for the Latin language.

Lemmas: The data was lemmatized with *Lemming* (Müller et al., 2015), a log-linear model of lemmatization making use of formal (edit trees between form and lemma, as well as affixes), lemma, part-of-speech and morphology and dictionary features (i.e. whether the lemma occurs in a list of pre-defined lemmas: for this I used the *Liddell-Scott-Jones* (LSJ) lexicon of Greek; Jones et al., 1996). Lemmatization accuracy was 0.969 initially; I was able to increase this to 0.980 by again using a *Morpheus* lexicon as a constraint, i.e. by restricting the output of *Lemming* to lemmas recognized by *Morpheus* as a valid lemma for the given Greek form/morphology-combination (if the form was recognized by *Morpheus*: otherwise, *Lemming* could freely decide upon a possible lemma). These results are higher than the state-of-the-art reported in Vatri and McGillivray (2020),[7] but the high accuracy is not completely unexpected, since in most cases only one option is possible due to the morphological complexity of Greek words. Accordingly, words that are not recognized by *Morpheus* have a significantly lower lemmatization accuracy (0.812). For the poetic data, lemmatization accuracy is a little lower than the prose data: accuracy ranges from 0.965 (comedies) to 0.975 (epic poetry) for the poetic data, while most prose genres have an accuracy of more than 0.980 (with oratory and biblical texts on the high end): see Table 4. The lemmas are generally consistent with the *LSJ* lexicon as well as

---

[7] They report lemmatization accuracies of 0.91 for a part of book 1 of the *Iliad* (with the CLTK backoff lemmatizer) and of 0.97 for *Lysias*, speech 7 (with the Diorisis lemmatizer). While the test set is different, *Lemming*'s lemmatization accuracy is 0.974 for the whole of the Iliad and 0.990 for all the Lysias data included in our treebank material. The results are not entirely comparable, however: our training set is different than the data that the tools used by Vatri and McGillivray (2020) are trained on, and we used the treebank material rather than our own annotation (as Vatri and McGillivray did) as a gold standard.

	Accuracy (N)
Biblical	0.989 (29,713)
Oratory	0.987 (19,876)
Dialogue	0.986 (998)
Biography	0.985 (10,655)
Military	0.985 (2,898)
Philosophical Dialogue	0.982 (3,576)
History	0.982 (73,278)
Rhetoric	0.981 (3,276)
Epistolography	0.980 (1,101)
Philosophical Treatise	0.980 (8,132)
Narrative Fiction	0.979 (8,392)
Epic Poetry	0.975 (42,836)
Papyri	0.972 (7,268)
Tragedy	0.972 (18,027)
Polyhistory	0.969 (8,095)
Lyric Poetry	0.967 (928)
Comedy	0.965 (4,650)

Table 4: Lemmatization accuracy by genre.

the lemmas included in the *Morpheus* codebase (which is largely based on *LSJ*).

Syntax: The *GLAUx* corpus was also annotated with dependency information consistent with the *AGDT* (2.0) guidelines, which are based on the annotation format of the *Prague Dependency Treebanks* (Böhmová et al., 2003). For this task the *Stanford Graph-Based Dependency Parser* (Dozat et al., 2017) proved suitable, a biaffine neural (LSTM) graph-based parser making use of character, token and part-of-speech embeddings. This parser was able to achieve a 0.845 labeled attachment score (LAS) for the papyri and a LAS ranging from 0.751 (philosophical and scientific prose) to 0.881 (biblical texts) for literary texts depending on text genre. Several remaining problems are caused by inconsistencies in the training and/or test data, which may be resolved by homogenization efforts (which we have already carried out in the past, and which we will also further carry out in the future). While the *AGDT* annotation format was used for historical reasons (most treebank projects of Greek are based on this format), in the future we plan to move to *UD* (Nivre et al., 2016), which is the annotation standard that is currently widely supported by the broader NLP community.

Semantics: Finally, *GLAUx* also includes semantic role annotation. For this task we had to develop our own annotation standard and training data, since there was relatively little semantically annotated data available, and the tag set of the *AGDT* for semantic annotation (Celano and Crane, 2015) was too fine-grained for automatic prediction and based on an old reference grammar that is not up-to-date with modern linguistic theory.[8] As the annotation was mainly done by job students, the semantic roles were based on the roles they were accustomed to, i.e. the ones developed for the pedagogical Pedalion project (Van Hal and Anné, 2017). However, this role set was expanded and revised to be compatible with a number of frameworks used for other languages as well (the description of arguments in particular remains rather underdeveloped in the Pedalion grammar), most importantly *VerbNet* (Kipper-Schuler, 2005) and *LIRICS* (Petukhova and Bunt, 2008). Currently 34 roles are distinguished (agent, beneficiary, cause, companion, comparison, concession, condition, degree, direction, duration, experiencer, extent of space, frequency, goal, identity, instrument, intermediary, location, maleficiary, manner, material, patient, possessor, property, recipient, respect, result, source, stimulus, theme, time, time frame, totality, value). For this purpose the semantic role labeler developed by Keersmaekers (2020a) was used, which makes use of a Random Forest classifier over a wide range of features (most importantly formal characteristics of the target word, its syntactic label, and lemma vectors of the target word and its head). This method was able to achieve an accuracy ranging from 0.687 for poetic texts to 0.838 for religious texts, with a relatively low number of training examples (about 12,500).

3 Problems

3.1 Text preservation and encoding textual variants

Many Greek texts have an intricate transmission history. Literary texts are typically transmitted through centuries of copying by medieval monks.

---

[8] For Latin, the *Index Thomisticus Treebank* also includes semantic role annotation based on the tectogrammatical layer of the Prague Dependency Treebanks (Passarotti, 2014), which is considerably more detailed than the role set used here (distinguishing 67 'functors').

Consequently, these texts do not have one version but multiple ones, as presented in the critical apparatus of the texts. Ideally, this critical apparatus would be directly encoded in the corpus, i.e. multiple versions of the same text would be aligned and each of these versions would be linguistically analyzed. In doing so, researchers will immediately know when encountering an unusual syntactic pattern whether there are any alternative readings or not (and, for example, be able to check whether the frequency of specific patterns remains the same if only words without alternative readings are taken into account). Unfortunately, the texts included in the *GLAUx* corpus are from a variety of sources that rarely include the critical apparatus. If more digital editions of critical apparatuses become available in the future, the quality of the *GLAUx* data will certainly be improved, but in the meantime *GLAUx* users should be aware that the underlying data is not always perfect (and might include some medieval alterations rather than actual language use in some cases).

The situation is different for the papyrological and epigraphical corpus, for which we have the original text as it was written in antiquity. This is not to say that no textual criticism is involved: firstly, some parts of the text may be harder to interpret or be entirely lost due to physical damage to the text material, in which case the interpretations of the editors of what this missing text should be (if such an interpretation is possible) can be considered a suggestion with which not everyone may agree. Secondly, the papyrological and epigraphic corpora have considerable spelling variation. For the papyrus corpus, editors usually standardize the spelling of papyrus texts, and these standardizations are included with the original forms in the XML version of the digital edition. For *GLAUx* we preserved both the 'original' and the 'standard' version for each word in the corpus (i.e. for a word like ἔχι which is an irregular spelling of ἔχει, both the forms 'ἔχι' and 'ἔχει' are included in the corpus). We based our automatic analysis on the standard version (in this case ἔχει), as the NLP tools we used were able to handle this version better (see also Keersmaekers 2020b: 12-14).

In addition, editors also often standardize morphology based on a classical norm, in which case performing the automatic analysis on the standard version is not advisable. In (1), for example, Μάρων (*Márōn*) is standardized by the editor to Μάρωνος (*Márōnos*). This is not based on phonological criteria, as there are no phonological reasons to omit the syllable -*os* at the ending of a word: rather the editor standardized the nominative Μάρων to the genitive Μάρωνος, as this case is normally expected after the preposition παρά (*pará*) "from". Labeling this word as a genitive based on the standard version would therefore misrepresent the case as it is actually used by the writer (which might be interesting from a diachronic perspective). Based on the lemma and morphological classification of the standard version, we therefore developed a rule-based system to generate this 'original' morphological information (e.g. when the standard version is a genitive on -ωνος and the original version is on -ων, and we know that the lemma belongs to the paradigm of words on -ων that have their genitive on -ωνος, we know that the correct case for the original version is a nominative).[9]

(1) ἀπέσταλκα δέ σοι τὸ δεῖγμα τοῦ παρὰ **Μάρων** (standardized to **Μάρωνος**) (P. Col. 3 51)
apéstalka dé soi tó deîgma toû pará **Márōn** (standardized to **Márōnos**)
I've sent you the sample from **Maron**.

Nevertheless, in some cases it is more difficult to decide whether we are dealing with phonological or morphological standardization: in (2), the use of the genitive σου (sou) where the editor expects the dative σοι (soi) – the standard expression of the recipient in Classical Greek – might be related to changes in case usage, but a phonological reason for the use of σου can also not be excluded, since the sounds of σου (/su/) and σοι (/sy/) are phonetically close to each other. For the current version of *GLAUx* we decided to include both a morphological analysis based on the original version (e.g. genitive in this example) and standard version (e.g. dative in this example), and leave a further classification which of these 'problems' are related to phonology and which ones to morphology for future research.

---

[9] This system builds on the work of Depauw and Stolk (2014), who have classified editorial regularizations for the papyri into broader categories (e.g. "ων instead of ωνος").

(2) δὸς τῷ κομείζοντί **σου** (standardized to
   σοι) τὴν ἐπιστολὴν (P. Oxy. 2 96)
   dós tô komeízontí **sou** (standardized to **soi**)
   tḗn epistolḗn
   Give to the person who has brought **you**
   the letter (…)

3.2 Extralinguistic variation

The Greek corpus is extremely diverse genre-wise, covers an extremely long time span, and the epigraphic corpus in particular also has considerable dialectal variation. This is, in the first place, a problem for automatic annotation: it is well known in NLP that accuracy drops when trying to analyze out-of-domain data, i.e. data that differs considerably from the training data. Not all these factors might be equally problematic: for the computational modelling of Greek lexical meaning, for example, McGillivray et al. (2019) found that genre is a more important factor than time, and argue that "literary Classical Greek is conservative when it comes to lexical semantics" (I also found similar results in my own experiments with meaning processing: see Keersmaekers 2020b: 119). As a complicating factor, there is a complex interplay between genre, diachrony and dialectal variation in literary Greek: some examples include Atticistic tendencies in post-classical Greek texts (i.e. imitating the prestige Athenian language variant of the fifth century BC) or the use of regional coloring tied to specific text types (e.g. the use of the Doric dialect in the chorus of tragedies, or an imitation of the Homeric dialect, which is already a mix of different dialects itself, in late epic poems).

There are several possible solutions to deal with this problem. One obvious solution is diversifying the training data. It has been shown by experiments on morphological tagging (Dik and Whaling, 2008) and syntactic parsing (Mambrini and Passarotti, 2012) of Ancient Greek that the quality of automatic annotation will significantly improve using in-domain data – similarly, I found that even a very small amount of papyrological training data could significantly improve the results for the automated analysis of these texts (Keersmaekers 2020b: 33). For the *Pedalion* treebanks which were included in the training data, we therefore aimed to include a variety of text types which are less well represented by the major treebanking projects (especially post-classical material), ranging from mathematical texts to private letters to horror stories.

Additionally, standardizing the training and/or test material during automatic analysis may also often lead to better results (see Piotrowski, 2012: 87): we have also taken some steps in this direction (see the use of standardized spelling as discussed in the previous section). Finally, in NLP several techniques have been developed to deal with out-of-domain labeling (e.g. Blitzer et al., 2006, Schnabel and Schütze, 2014). For syntactic parsing, I will experiment with the use of treebank embeddings (Stymne et al., 2018) in the future, which have shown to handle heterogeneous data well. An open question with the use of these techniques is which texts constitute the given domain that our NLP models should be adapted to (i.e. given a certain text type such as papyrus letters, which training data should be considered 'in-domain' and which 'out-of-domain'), given the complex interactions between genre, diachrony and dialect outlined above. Possibly text similarity measures (see Turney and Pantel, 2010) may provide valuable insights in this respect.

A more fundamental question is whether it is advisable to use a single annotation format for such a diverse corpus. On the one hand, several NLP projects such as *UD* (Nivre et al., 2016) have developed an annotation format for even broader purposes (covering all natural languages), and one could argue that the categories used in part-of-speech tagging and syntactic parsing are broad enough not to be affected by language variation too much (while semantic annotation should, ideally, be universal). On the other hand, the *GLAUx* corpus includes a large number of 'languages' as 'Greek', which may in some cases very strongly differ from each other (e.g. the language of mathematical texts vs. epic poems): researchers such as Haspelmath (2010) and Croft (2013) have also argued against the generalizability of linguistic categories. In a practical sense, this issue might be resolved by detailed annotation documentation of constructions that are highly peculiar to a particular text genre: expanding the manually annotated treebank data to more 'unusual' text genres, as discussed above, is obviously highly beneficial for identifying such constructions.

3.3 Linguistic ambiguity and historical change

It is well known that linguistic ambiguity is an important factor in diachronical change: change often happens in 'bridging contexts', i.e. contexts that are ambiguous between two constructions (Heine, 2002; Eckardt, 2006; Traugott, 2012). For example, the Greek word ἵνα (*hina*) develops from a conjunction introducing a purpose clause, as in (3), to a complementizer, as in (4). Ambiguous examples such as (5), in which the ἵνα-clause could either be interpreted as a complement clause or a purpose clause, may have caused this change. At any rate, such examples are highly problematic for the annotation format of the *AGDT*, in which a strict distinction is made between complement clauses and adverbial clauses.

> (3) ἐντεῖλαι περὶ τούτου Κράτωνι **ἵνα** μὴ πάλιν σκυλῆτε με ἀναβῆναι πρὸς ὑμᾶς. (P. Strasb. 5 346)
>
> enteîlai perí toútou Krátōni **hína** mé pálin skulête me anabênai prós humâs.
>
> Give orders for this to Kraton, **so that** you do not force (?) me again to come to you.

> (4) Ὠφελίωνι ἐνετειλάμην **ἵνα** καὶ αὐτὸς δοῖ ἑτέραν καὶ τοὺς ἄρτους μοι πέμψηι. (P. Ryl. 2 229)
>
> ōphelíōni eneteilámēn **hína** kaí autos doî hetéran kaí toús ártous moi pémpsēi.
>
> I have ordered Ophelion **to** give you another one and to send me the loaves of bread.

> (5) ἔντειλαι τῶι παρά σου, **ἵνα** τὸ τάχος γέ[νη]ται. (PSI 4 326)
>
> énteilai tōi pará sou, **hína** tó tákhos génētai.
>
> Give commands to your messager "**in order that** there will be haste" or "**that** there should be haste"

When performing automatic annotation, such ambiguities may be reflected in the underlying probabilities of the natural language processing model: example (5) shares features both of a prototypical adverbial clause (e.g. unlike in (4), the subject of the ἵνα-clause and the recipient of the command are different entities) and a prototypical complement clause (the verb ἐντέλλω *entéllō*

"command" typically requires an argument expressing the command), which should in principle be learnable by a NLP system if the relevant features are annotated. Hence when automatically labelling clauses for the adverbial/complement distinction, I found that clauses with high predicted probabilities of being a complement showed very prototypical features of complement clauses and vice versa for adverbial clauses (although the cases with 'in-between' probabilities showed a mix of complement, adverbial and ambiguous examples: see Keersmaekers 2020b: 158-174 for more detail). While corpus projects often simply only include the most probable label in their annotation, this underlying probability distribution may offer valuable information to detect such 'less prototypical' cases (although the output probabilities are obviously highly dependent on the quality of the automatic technique and the feature set it is provided with). For reasons of transparency I will therefore make as much information about the automatic prediction publicly available as possible.[10]

4 Conclusion and outlook

This paper has described *GLAUx*, an ongoing project aiming to compile a large and diverse corpus of historical Greek. A test version of this corpus has already been released on GitHub:[11] we aim to release a first version including all the papyrus data and the literary data until the fourth century AD in the course of 2021. I identified some important issues in constructing this corpus, and suggested a number of possible solutions: these include the encoding of textual variants, dealing with a high degree of extralinguistic variation and annotating 'ambiguous' constructions. These issues should be highly relevant for other researchers working with historical corpora, and I hope that this discussion may inspire further research.

The annotation of this corpus will be continuously improved in the coming years, as it is put to work in several research projects at the KU Leuven. It plays a key role in the pedagogical Pedalion project [12] and in a recently approved

---

[10] While this section mainly discussed label ambiguities, syntactic head attachment may also be ambiguous: see e.g. McGillivray and Vatri, 2015 for a discussion on how to resolve such ambiguities. Again, automatic methods could be suitable to detect such ambiguities, if the right features (e.g.

valency and prosodical information, as discussed by McGillivray and Vatri) are provided.

[11] https://github.com/perseids-publications/glaux-trees

[12] http://www.pedalion.be

research project entitled *Language and Ideas: Towards a New Computational and Corpus-Based Approach to Ancient Greek Semantics and the History of Ideas* (FWO, Research Foundation – Flanders, grant number 3H200733). In this project we will examine how the *GLAUx* corpus can be applied to the study of language-related ideas expressed in Ancient Greek. The underlying hypothesis is that applying well-informed corpus-based methods, going beyond the level of the individual word or term, enables us to study (intellectual and conceptual) history from a wider perspective. It goes without saying that the applications for other domains and projects are manifold.

Some short-term enhancements we are planning include improving the underlying NLP work (in particular, we are currently exploring the possibilities of training an *ELECTRA* transformer model: see Clark et al., 2020), the addition of a derivational annotation layer and changing the syntactic annotation format to *Universal Dependencies*. In the long term, we will also expand *GLAUx* with the epigraphical data and develop techniques to handle the peculiarities of these texts, and expand the literary data up until the eighth century AD. To improve the accessibility of the data, we are currently designing detailed documentation about the different annotation layers of *GLAUx*, and will also provide a user interface to query the data.

All the data provided for *GLAUx* will be openly released online. We are currently discussing collaboration opportunities with other major digital projects of Greek, including the *Open Greek and Latin* project[13] and Trismegistos[14], so as to expand the possibilities for digital approaches to Ancient Greek as much as possible in the near future.

Acknowledgments

The work described in this paper has its basis in the Natural Language Processing and corpus design work I carried out during my PhD (funded by FWO, Research Foundation – Flanders, grant number 1162017N), which was supervised by Dirk Speelman, Toon Van Hal and Mark Depauw, as well as a one-year project funded by KU Leuven.[15] Mark Depauw has also considerably assisted me with the papyrus part of this corpus, and Toon Van Hal with the literary part. Currently the underlying NLP work is also further being improved through the help of Wouter Mercelis. I would also like to thank the three anonymous reviewers and the workshop organizers for their feedback, which has greatly helped to improve the quality of this paper. Lastly, the work described in this paper would not have been possible without the immense effort of various corpus annotators (including our own job students at KU Leuven) to provide a large amount of manually annotated data for Greek which this project has used as training data.

References

David Bamman, Francesco Mambrini, and Gregory Crane. 2009. An ownership model of annotation: The Ancient Greek dependency treebank. In *Proceedings of the Eighth International Workshop on Treebanks and Linguistic Theories (TLT 8)*, pages 5–15, Milan. EDUCatt: Ente per il Diritto allo Studio Universitario dell'Università Cattolic. https://convegni.unicatt.it/meetings_Proceedings_TLT8.pdf.

John Blitzer, Ryan McDonald, and Fernando Pereira. 2006. Domain Adaptation with Structural Correspondence Learning. In *Proceedings of the 2006 Conference on Empirical Methods in Natural Language Processing*, pages 120–128, Sydney. Association for Computational Linguistics. https://www.aclweb.org/anthology/W06-1615.

Alena Böhmová, Jan Hajič, Eva Hajičová, and Barbora Hladká. 2003. The Prague dependency treebank. In Anne Abeillé, editor, *Treebanks: Building and Using Parsed Corpora*, Text, Speech and Language Technology 20, pages 103–127. Springer, New York. https://doi.org/10.1007/978-94-010-0201-1_7.

Bernd Bohnet and Joakim Nivre. 2012. A Transition-Based System for Joint Part-of-Speech Tagging and Labeled Non-Projective Dependency Parsing. In *Proceedings of the 2012 Joint Conference on Empirical Methods in Natural Language Processing and Computational Natural Language Learning*, pages 1455–1465, Jeju Island, Korea. Association for Computational Linguistics. https://www.aclweb.org/anthology/D12-1133.

Hugh A. Cayless, James M.S. Cowey, Ryan Baumman, and Timothy David Hill. 2021. Papyri.info IDP (Integrating Digital Papyrology) Data. https://github.com/papyri/idp.data.

---

[13] https://www.opengreekandlatin.org
[14] https://www.trismegistos.org

[15] https://www.kuleuven.be/onderzoek/portaal/#/projecten/3H200333

Giuseppe G. A. Celano. 2017. Lemmatized Ancient Greek Texts. https://github.com/gcelano /LemmatizedAncientGreekXML.

Giuseppe G. A. Celano. 2018. An Automatic Morphological Annotation and Lemmatization for the IDP Papyri. In Nicola Reggiani, editor, *Digital Papyrology II: Case Studies on the Digital Edition of Ancient Greek Papyri*, pages 139–147. De Gruyter Open Access Books, Berlin, Boston. https://doi.org/10.1515/9783110547450-008.

Giuseppe G. A. Celano and Gregory Crane. 2015. Semantic role annotation in the ancient greek dependency treebank. In Markus Dickinson, Erhard Hinrichs, Agnieszka Patejuk, and Adam Przepiórkowski, editors, *Proceedings of the Fourteenth International Workshop on Treebanks and Linguistic Theories (TLT14)*, pages 26–34, Warsaw. Polish Academy of Sciences, Institute of Computer Science. http://tlt14.ipipan.waw.pl/files /4614/5063/3858/TLT14_proceedings.pdf.

Kevin Clark, Minh-Thang Luong, Quoc V. Le, and Christopher D. Manning. 2020. *ELECTRA: Pre-training Text Encoders as Discriminators Rather Than Generators*. arXiv:2003.10555.

Ronan Collobert, Jason Weston, Léon Bottou, Michael Karlen, Koray Kavukcuoglu, and Pavel Kuksa. 2011. Natural language processing (almost) from scratch. *Journal of machine learning research*, 12:2493–2537. https://www.jmlr.org/papers /volume12/collobert11a/collobert11a.pdf.

Gregory Crane. 1991. Generating and parsing classical Greek. *Literary and Linguistic Computing*, 6(4):243–245. https://doi.org/10.1093/llc/6.4.243.

Gregory Crane. 2021. Perseus Digital Library. https://github.com/PerseusDL/canonical-greekLit.

Gregory Crane, Lenny Muellner, Bruce Robertson, Alison Babeu, Lisa Cerrato, Thomas Koentges, Rhea Lesage, Lucie Stylianopoulos, and James Tauber. 2021. First1KGreek. https://opengreekandlatin.github.io/First1KGreek.

William Croft. 2013. Radical Construction Grammar. In Thomas Hoffmann and Graeme Trousdale, editors, *The Oxford Handbook of Construction Grammar*, pages 211–232. Oxford University Press, Oxford. https://doi.org/10.1093/oxfordhb /9780195396683.013.0012.

Francesca Dell'Oro and Giuseppe GA Celano. 2019. Epigraphic Treebanks: Some Considerations from a Work in Progress. *Classics@(First Drafts@)*. https://chs.harvard.edu/wp-content/uploads/2020 /11/DellOroCelano_4.pdf.

Mark Depauw and Tom Gheldof. 2014. Trismegistos: An Interdisciplinary Platform for Ancient World Texts and Related Information. In Łukasz Bolikowski, Vittore Casarosa, Paula Goodale, Nikos Houssos, Paolo Manghi, and Jochen Schirrwagen, editors, *Theory and Practice of Digital Libraries -- TPDL 2013 Selected Workshops*, pages 40–52, Cham. Springer International Publishing. https://doi.org/10.1007 /978-3-319-08425-1_5.

Mark Depauw and Joanne Stolk. 2014. Linguistic variation in Greek papyri: Towards a new tool for quantitative study. *Greek, Roman, and Byzantine Studies*, 55(1):196–220. https://grbs.library.duke.edu/article/view/15245/65 61.

Helma Dik and Richard Whaling. 2008. Bootstrapping Classical Greek Morphology. In *Digital Humanities 2008*, pages 105–106, Oulu. Association for Literary and Linguistic Computing, Association for Computers and the Humanities and Society for Digital Humanities. http://www.ekl.oulu.fi/dh2008 /Digital%20Humanities%202008%20Book%20of %20Abstracts.pdf.

Timothy Dozat, Peng Qi, and Christopher D. Manning. 2017. Stanford's Graph-based Neural Dependency Parser at the CoNLL 2017 Shared Task. In *Proceedings of the CoNLL 2017 Shared Task: Multilingual Parsing from Raw Text to Universal Dependencies*, pages 20–30, Vancouver. Association for Computational Linguistics. https://doi.org/10.18653/v1/K17-3002.

Regine Eckardt. 2006. *Meaning Change in Grammaticalization: An Enquiry into Semantic Reanalysis*. Oxford University Press, Oxford. https://doi.org/10.1093/acprof:oso/9780199262601 .001.0001.

Vanessa B. Gorman. 2020. Dependency Treebanks of Ancient Greek Prose. *Journal of Open Humanities Data*, 6(1). https://doi.org/10.5334/johd.13.

Stefan Th. Gries, Tobias Bernaisch, and Benedikt Heller. 2018. A corpus-linguistic account of the history of the genitive alternation in Singapore English. In Sandra C. Deshors, editor, *Modeling World Englishes: Assessing the interplay of emancipation and globalization of ESL varieties*, Varieties of English Around the World, pages 245–280. John Benjamins Publishing Company, Amsterdam; Philadelphia. https://doi.org/10.1075 /veaw.g61.10gri.

Martin Haspelmath. 2010. Comparative concepts and descriptive categories in crosslinguistic studies. *Language*, 86(3):663–687. https://doi.org/10.1353 /lan.2010.0021.

Dag TT Haug and Marius Jøhndal. 2008. Creating a parallel treebank of the old Indo-European Bible translations. In Caroline Sporleder and Kiril Ribarov, editors, *Proceedings of the second workshop on language technology for cultural heritage data (LaTeCH 2008)*, pages 27–34, Marrakech. http://www.lrec-conf.org/proceedings /lrec2008/workshops/W22_Proceedings.pdf.

Bernd Heine. 2002. On the Role of Context in Grammaticalization. In Ilse Wischer and Gabriele Diewald, editors, *New Reflections on Grammaticalization*, Typological Studies in Language 49, pages 83–101. Benjamins, Amsterdam. https://doi.org/10.1075/tsl.49.08hei.

Paul A. Iversen. 2007. The Packard Humanities Institute (PHI) Greek Epigraphy Project and the Revolution in Greek Epigraphy. Abgadiyat, 2(1):51–55.

Henry Stuart Jones, Henry George Liddell, Roderick MacKenzie, Robert Scott, and A. A. Thompson. 1996. *A Greek-English Lexicon*. Clarendon, Oxford, New ed. with new supplement edition.

Alek Keersmaekers. 2020a. Automatic semantic role labeling in Ancient Greek using distributional semantic modeling. In *Proceedings of LT4HALA 2020 - 1st Workshop on Language Technologies for Historical and Ancient Languages*, pages 59–67, Marseille. European Language Resources Association (ELRA). https://www.aclweb.org /anthology/2020.lt4hala-1.9.

Alek Keersmaekers. 2020b. *A computational approach to the Greek papyri: developing a corpus to study variation and change in the post-classical Greek complementation system*. Ph.D. thesis, KU Leuven. https://lirias.kuleuven.be/3084305.

Alek Keersmaekers, Wouter Mercelis, Colin Swaelens, and Toon Van Hal. 2019. Creating, Enriching and Valorizing Treebanks of Ancient Greek. In *Proceedings of the 18th International Workshop on Treebanks and Linguistic Theories (TLT, SyntaxFest 2019)*, pages 109–117, Paris, August. Association for Computational Linguistics (ACL). https://doi.org/10.18653/v1/W19-7812.

Karin Kipper-Schuler. 2005. *VerbNet: A broad-coverage, comprehensive verb lexicon*. Ph.D. thesis, University of Pennsylvania. https://repository.upenn.edu/dissertations/AAI3179 808.

Andrey Kutuzov, Lilja Øvrelid, Terrence Szymanski, and Erik Velldal. 2018. Diachronic word embeddings and semantic shifts: a survey. In *Proceedings of the 27th International Conference on Computational Linguistics*, pages 1384–1397, Santa Fe, New Mexico. Association for Computational Linguistics. https://www.aclweb.org /anthology/C18-1117.

Eleonora Litta, Marco Passarotti, and Francesco Mambrini. 2019. The Treatment of Word Formation in the LiLa Knowledge Base of Linguistic Resources for Latin. In *Proceedings of the Second International Workshop on Resources and Tools for Derivational Morphology*, pages 35–43, Prague, Czechia, September. Charles University, Faculty of Mathematics and Physics, Institute of Formal and Applied Linguistics. https://www.aclweb.org /anthology/W19-8505.

Francesco Mambrini and Marco Carlo Passarotti. 2012. Will a parser overtake Achilles? First experiments on parsing the ancient Greek dependency treebank. In *Proceedings of the Eleventh International Workshop on Treebanks and Linguistic Theories*, pages 133–144. Edições Colibri. https://publicatt.unicatt.it/handle/10807 /37956.

Barbara McGillivray, Simon Hengchen, Viivi Lähteenoja, Marco Palma, and Alessandro Vatri. 2019. A computational approach to lexical polysemy in Ancient Greek. *Digital Scholarship in the Humanities*, 34(4):893–907. https://doi.org /10.1093/llc/fqz036.

Barbara McGillivray and Alessandro Vatri. 2015. Computational valency lexica for Latin and Greek in use: a case study of syntactic ambiguity. *Journal of Latin Linguistics*, 14(1):101–126. https://doi.org /10.1515/joll-2015-0005.

Thomas Müller, Ryan Cotterell, Alexander Fraser, and Hinrich Schütze. 2015. Joint Lemmatization and Morphological Tagging with Lemming. In *Proceedings of the 2015 Conference on Empirical Methods in Natural Language Processing*, pages 2268–2274, Lisbon. Association for Computational Linguistics. https://doi.org/10.18653/v1/D15-1272.

Joakim Nivre, Marie-Catherine De Marneffe, Filip Ginter, Yoav Goldberg, Jan Hajic, Christopher D. Manning, Ryan McDonald, Slav Petrov, Sampo Pyysalo, and Natalia Silveira. 2016. Universal dependencies v1: A multilingual treebank collection. In *Proceedings of the Tenth International Conference on Language Resources and Evaluation (LREC'16)*, pages 1659–1666. https://www.aclweb.org/anthology/L16-1262.

Maria C. Pantelia. 2021. Thesaurus Linguae Graecae® Digital Library. http://www.tlg.uci.edu.

Marco Passarotti. 2014. From Syntax to Semantics. First Steps Towards Tectogrammatical Annotation of Latin. In *Proceedings of the 8th Workshop on Language Technology for Cultural Heritage, Social Sciences, and Humanities (LaTeCH)*, pages 100–109, Gothenburg. Association for Computational Linguistics. https://doi.org/10.3115/v1/W14-0615.

Florent Perek and Martin Hilpert. 2017. A distributional semantic approach to the periodization of change in the productivity of constructions. *International journal of corpus linguistics*, 22(4):490–520. https://doi.org/10.1075/ijcl.16128.per.

Volha Petukhova and Harry Bunt. 2008. LIRICS Semantic Role Annotation: Design and Evaluation of a Set of Data Categories. In *Proceedings of the Sixth International Conference on Language Resources and Evaluation (LREC '08)*, Marrakech. European Language Resources Association (ELRA). https://www.aclweb.org/anthology/L08-1428.

Michael Piotrowski. 2012. *Natural language processing for historical texts*. Synthesis lectures on human language technologies. Morgan & Claypool, San Rafael, California. https://doi.org/10.2200/S00436ED1V01Y201207HLT017.

Helmut Schmid. 1994. Probabilistic part-of-speech tagging using decision trees. In *Proceedings of the International Conference on New Methods in Language Processing*, pages 44–49, Manchester.

Helmut Schmid and Florian Laws. 2008. Estimation of Conditional Probabilities With Decision Trees and an Application to Fine-Grained POS Tagging. In *Proceedings of the 22nd International Conference on Computational Linguistics (Coling 2008)*, pages 777–784, Manchester. Coling 2008 Organizing Committee. https://www.aclweb.org/anthology/C08-1098.

Tobias Schnabel and Hinrich Schütze. 2014. FLORS: Fast and Simple Domain Adaptation for Part-of-Speech Tagging. *Transactions of the Association for Computational Linguistics*, 2:15–26. https://doi.org/10.1162/tacl_a_00162.

Sara Stymne, Miryam de Lhoneux, Aaron Smith, and Joakim Nivre. 2018. Parser Training with Heterogeneous Treebanks. In *Proceedings of the 56th Annual Meeting of the Association for Computational Linguistics (Volume 2: Short Papers)*, pages 619–625, Melbourne. Association for Computational Linguistics. https://doi.org/10.18653/v1/P18-2098.

Elizabeth Closs Traugott. 2012. The Status of Onset Contexts in Analysis of Micro-Changes. In Merja Kytö, editor, *English Corpus Linguistics: Crossing Paths*, Language and Computers, pages 221–255. Rodopi, Amsterdam. https://doi.org/10.1163/9789401207935_012.

Peter D. Turney and Patrick Pantel. 2010. From frequency to meaning: Vector space models of semantics. *Journal of artificial intelligence research*, 37:141–188. https://doi.org/10.1613/jair.2934.

Toon Van Hal and Yannick Anné. 2017. Reconciling the dynamics of language with a grammar handbook: The ongoing Pedalion grammar project. *Digital Scholarship in the Humanities*, 32(2):448–454. https://doi.org/10.1093/llc/fqv068.

Alessandro Vatri and Barbara McGillivray. 2018. The Diorisis Ancient Greek Corpus. *Research Data Journal for the Humanities and Social Sciences*, 3(1):55–65. https://doi.org/10.1163/24523666-01000013.

Alessandro Vatri and Barbara McGillivray. 2020. Lemmatization for Ancient Greek: An experimental assessment of the state of the art. *Journal of Greek Linguistics*, 20(2):179–196. https://doi.org/10.1163/15699846-02002001.

Bhāṣācitra: Visualising the dialect geography of South Asia

Aryaman Arora
Georgetown University
aa2190@georgetown.edu

Adam Farris
San Mateo High School
adamfarris@gmail.com

Gopalakrishnan R
EFL University, Hyderabad
gopalkrishnan11251@gmail.com

Samopriya Basu
University of North Carolina – Chapel Hill
sampr0b@live.unc.edu

Abstract

We present Bhāṣācitra,[1] a dialect mapping system for South Asia built on a database of linguistic studies of languages of the region annotated for topic and location data. We analyse language coverage and look towards applications to typology by visualising example datasets. The application is not only meant to be useful for feature mapping, but also serves as a new kind of interactive bibliography for linguists of South Asian languages.

1 Introduction

South Asia is extremely linguistically diverse. There is a common saying illustrating this diversity, present in several languages of the region; it is given in Hindi below.

> *kos kos par pānī badle, cār kos par bānī.*
> 'The taste of water changes every mile,
> and the language every four.'

One issue with this vast scale of diversity is the difficulty it poses for linguists in collecting and cataloguing linguistic data, which further impedes comprehensive typological analysis. India alone contains known living speakers of 461 languages (Eberhard et al., 2021).[2] It is also difficult to assess the availability of linguistic literature for all of these languages, leading to gaps in the typological databases we end up compiling; print linguistic bibliographies for the region become outdated as new work is published and do not encode useful metadata, such as the specific dialect studied in each work or the linguistic features studied.

In this paper we present **Bhāṣācitra**, a database of linguistic sources for South Asian languages

that we have compiled and annotated, as well as a dialect mapping and visualising system built from the location data extracted from those sources. Currently it includes 1104 labelled sources covering 311 lects. The site is online at http://aryamanarora.github.io/bhasacitra.

2 Background and related work

Dialects[3] are defined by *isoglosses*, geographical boundaries separating linguistic features. The mapping of dialect geography is a well-established problem in linguistics, and has been done for many languages; two illustrative examples are English (Orton et al., 1998; Kretzschmar, 2001) and Japanese (Kumagai, 2016). Dialect mapping is instrumentally important for the study of historical–comparative linguistics, since the present-day geography of isoglosses is a result of past *language change* and *language contact*. The distribution of synchronic features is data for theories of diachronic language change.

Computational approaches to dialect geography have worked on many parts of the issue, including the compilation of broad databases of linguistic features (Dryer and Haspelmath, 2013; Carling et al., 2018), dialect identification and clustering on modern social media corpora (Abdul-Mageed et al., 2018; Jones, 2015), and statistical modelling of dialect groups (e.g. Murawaki, 2020).

South Asia is a *linguistic area* (Masica, 1993; Bashir, 2016), a region of typological convergence due to historical contact between speakers of languages of different families. Families represented

---

[1] From Sanskrit *bhāṣā* 'language' + *citra* 'ornament, appearence'; lit. 'language map'.

[2] But note Asher (2008): "It is impossible to be at all precise about either the number of languages spoken in the region or the number of speakers of each."

[3] *Dialect* for the purposes of this paper refers to any speech variety. South Asia as a region is prone, due to geographical and historical factors, to fuzzy boundaries between speech varieties. The situation is best explained by Deo (2018) in describing the distribution of Indo-Aryan as "sociolinguistically rich and complex, characterized by plurilinguality and dialect continua spread over large regions spanning multiple languages".

Proceedings of the 2nd International Workshop on Computational Approaches to Historical Language Change 2021, pages 51–57
August 6, 2021. ©2021 Association for Computational Linguistics

Figure 1: The primary interface map for Bhāṣācitra generated with D3.js and Voronoi partitioning.

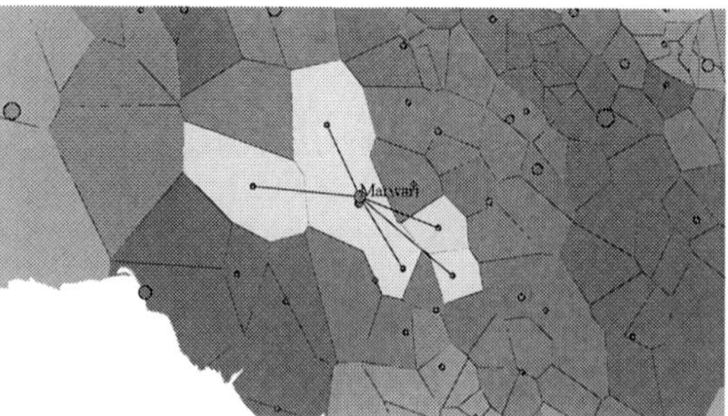

Figure 2: Hovering on the circle for Marwari (a language of Rajasthan, India) highlights the regions from which linguistic sources for it draw data.

in South Asia are Indo-European, Dravidian, Austroasiatic, Sino-Tibetan, and some unclassified isolates (Nihali, Kusunda, and Burushaski).

Visualisation of data for linguistic typology has a long history, beginning with the first lexical isogloss maps created by aggregating data from dialect surveys and with more recent work specifically for visualising historical change, such as Kalouli et al. (2019). As linguists adopt computational methods that deal with vast amounts of data, it becomes a challenge for humans to interpret datasets. Modern approaches to visualisation like Visual Analytics (VA) try to address this issue (Keim et al., 2008; MacEachren, 2017).

The use of point-based mapping in linguistic data visualisation is well-known, in e.g. WALS (Dryer and Haspelmath, 2013). This format has been used to map data in South Asian languages (Arsenault, 2017; Liljegren et al., 2021) as well as the languages of Iran (Anonby et al., 2019, 2018). We develop this paradigm further to map areal language extents based on the location data in published linguistic fieldwork.

3 Data model

We built Bhāṣācitra to be an easy-to-use system for researchers with no computational background. We implemented the application in JavaScript on a statically-hosted webpage. There are three data files in JSON format, for reference metadata (in

BibTeX-compatible format with additional fields for location and topic information; see appendix A), language metadata (traditional genetic classification and coordinates for reference locations), and the typological database (containing per-language per-location data).

The primary interface is an interactive map displaying geographical points corresponding to locations from which language data has been collected. The map is generated and manipulated using the D3.js library which has a complete pipeline for web cartography (Bostock et al., 2011). Dialect zones are partitioned using the Voronoi algorithm; for a point P_k in the set of points P, its Voronoi region R_k is defined as all points closer to P_k than to any other point.

$$R_k = \left\{ x \in X \;\middle|\; \arg\min_i \left(\text{dist}(P_i, x) \right) = k \right\} \quad (1)$$

In the primary interface (see figure 3), zones are colour-coded by consensus genetic classification of the languages covering the zone, with circles (with size proportional to the number of sources) centered at the weighted average of the coordinates of descriptions of the languages. In the case where multiple languages share a zone, the RGB components of the colouring are averaged.

3.1 Interface

The primary interface map is fully interactive (draggable and zoomable). Hovering over a language circle shows all the geographical points and Voronoi polygons associated with the sources compiled for that language (see figure 2). Like the language circles, each geographical point's size is weighted by the number of sources corresponding to it. Clicking on a language circle brings up the scrollable bibliography for that language, with each entry in

Topic	Count
overview (descriptive grammars)	494
syntax	141
phonetics/phonology	125
historical	111
morphology	100
sociolinguistics	91
lexicography	83
corpora	51
dialectology	48
comparative	44
Total	1104

Table 1: Count of sources labelled under the top 10 topics. A single source can be labelled with multiple topics.

human-readable format with the corresponding location and topic annotations appended.

3.2 Limitations

In South Asia (as elsewhere), geography is hardly the only variable encoding language use. As noted by Deo (2018) and shown in sociolinguistic studies (Gumperz, 1958) factors such as caste, social status, political affiliation, and religion play a large role in language use and adoption. Migrant speaker communities have also developed distinct dialects even in regions where they are a minority language group (e.g. Marathi speakers in Thanjavur and Burushaski speakers in Srinagar).

To deal with geographical overlap (different language sources for the same location), we allowed the areal zones of multiple languages to encompass the same location. A complete solution to the limitations of the geographical model would require collection of demographic data indexed to language use, which has not yet been collected on a large scale in South Asia.

4 Compiling the database

There are some existing bibliographies of language references for South Asia. In compiling data for Bhāṣācitra, we prioritised the incorporation of sources that provided the greatest coverage of language information, such as grammars and grammatical sketches, analysed corpora, and sociolinguistic surveys.

We began with data from Glottolog for broad coverage (Hammarström et al., 2020); South Asia-specific sources we drew from are Peterson (2018); Baart and Baart-Bremer (2001); Perera (2021). We then searched for literature not included in existing bibliographies. Many new sources were obtained

Figure 3: Map of all locations extracted from the sources in the Bhāṣācitra database.

from Shodhganga,[4] a platform for open-access digitised theses completed at Indian universities. These theses were difficult to access before the past decade, so from this resource we were able to incorporate many new references.

We annotated information on topic coverage for every source (see table 1) and location data (see §4.1) when possible. We also preferred to link to open-access versions of sources. In total, we compiled **1104 sources** describing **311 lects** with data collected from **763 locations**. This number is continually increasing as we actively improve our coverage of the linguistic literature and new work is published.

4.1 Locations

The primary new contribution of the Bhāṣācitra database is location data manually collected from the included references, shown in figure 3. The geocoding of the locations was done through the Google Maps API and manually verified.

While databases such as Glottolog and WALS do include location data for languages, their representation reduces the language's geographical distribution to a single point. We instead represent multiple points per language based on data from the sources we catalogued.

For example, in Glottolog, Hindi is placed at a single point in central India, whereas in Bhāṣācitra there are 21 locations associated with Hindi–Urdu, with most sources describing the standard dialect in Delhi, but also work dealing with varieties in Varanasi, Lahore, and the rural regions surrounding Delhi. Areal mapping of linguistic references allows for better assessment of the coverage of dialects in our sources, and for explicit coverage of dialect variation when mapping features.

---

[4] https://shodhganga.inflibnet.ac.in/

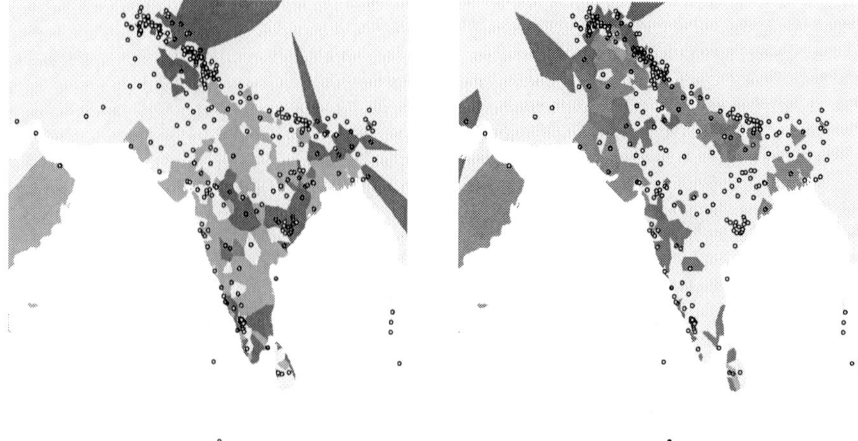

(a) Distribution of the breathy-voiced retroflex stop (/ɖʱ/) in South Asian languages.

(b) Percent of sound changes of Sanskrit /kṣ/ that result in /k(ː)ʰ/ in various Indo-Aryan languages.

Figure 4: Example datasets mapped in Bhāṣācitra. Scale: Yes/100%, No/0%

5 Mapping datasets

To illustrate the value of areal visualisation of language features, we mapped two datasets: the phoneme inventories of a large number of Indian languages from Ramaswami (1999), and the outcomes of selected sound changes from Sanskrit to the modern Indo-Aryan languages based on the Jambu database (Arora and Farris, 2021) parsed from Turner (1962–1966).

Note that we only visually analyse the map in these examples; these observations would need to be corroborated with statistic analysis and modelling to result in any verifiable claims.

5.1 Phoneme inventories

From the data in Ramaswami (1999) collected in the PHOIBLE database (Moran and McCloy, 2019) we were able to map the phoneme inventories of 62 major South Asian languages. Several works have studied the phonetic typology of the South Asian linguistic area, e.g. Ramanujan and Masica (2016); Arsenault (2017), but have not used areal mapping visualisations.

Some interesting phonological features for mapping are retroflexion (which is prevalent throughout the region, but weakly distinguished or not distinguished at all in the eastern periphery) and breathy-voiced stops (which are less common in much of the Dravidian and Munda families and in the northwestern languages). Figure 4a shows the distribution of the breathy-voiced retroflex stop /ɖʱ/ (in IAST: ḍh) using the Bhāṣācitra system.

While Arsenault (2017) did use mapping, the feature-separating lines were calculated based on point coordinates for each language, not areal zones. Bhāṣācitra produces more accurate visualisations; it is immediately clear that the northwest Indo-Aryan and Nuristani, Dravidian, and Munda languages lack the phoneme, and this information can be used to inform locations for future fieldwork at the isogloss boundaries to refine our data.

5.2 Indo-Aryan sound changes

As another demonstration, we use an under-development etymological database of Indo-Aryan languages (Arora and Farris, 2021) that builds on Turner (1962–1966) to map the outcomes of some key Indo-Aryan sound changes.[5]

The Indo-Aryan (IA) languages show complex overlapping phonological isoglosses as a symptom of intense cross-dialectal contact over a long period of time, whose complexity makes it difficult to make sense of the family's linguistic history. For example, the Sanskrit cluster /kṣ/ generally develops to /kʰ/ in the core region of modern Indo-Aryan and /t͡ʃʰ/ in the periphery, but some doublets are evidence of dialect contact, e.g. Sanskrit /kṣaːrə/ > Hindi /t͡ʃʰaːr/ 'ashes' as well as /kʰaːr/ 'alkali' (Masica, 1993). The variability of these sound changes has recently been used

---

[5]The compilation of the Jambu database is not in the scope of this work, but, briefly, it has been compiled by parsing data from the digitised version of Turner (1962–1966) and augmenting it with several more recent diachronic dictionaries for Indo-Aryan languages.

to statistically model dialect components in IA languages (Cathcart, 2019a,b, 2020; Cathcart and Rama, 2020).

Thus, a visualisation of the probability of certain IA sound changes based on a lexical database would be useful for finding isoglosses and the geographical extent of historical dialect contact. We aligned the cognate forms given in Arora and Farris (2021) using the LingPy library's multiple alignment function (List et al., 2019). Based on the alignments, the likelihood of $/k\d{s}/ > /k(\textlengthmark)^h/$ is mapped in figure 4b. A rough core–periphery distinction indeed emerges, with languages in the northwest, south, and east having fewer outcomes of $/k(\textlengthmark)^h/$. It is also apparent that the language coverage in Turner (1962–1966) is limited, with a great deal of core IA languages lacking data.

6   Future work

We intend to maximise coverage of South Asian languages in Bhāṣācitra. In the interest of achieving this goal we welcome contributions to our open-source database on GitHub: `https://github.com/aryamanarora/bhasacitra`. Ultimately, this sort of database would be useful for all languages of the world, but we lack the domain knowledge for non-South Asian languages, so we welcome any collaborators who feel this system would be beneficial.

As for directions for technical work, Bhāṣācitra would benefit from a SQL database for faster querying and precomputation of some data (e.g. language circle sizes and coordinates) to improve performance in the browser. In the interface, we will explore continuous alternatives to discretised Voronoi polygons, which force rigid transitions between lects[6] and do not show where location coverage is sparse. This will also help us with the issue of large polygons at the edges of our research area. Also, a basemap with administrative boundaries and other contextual geographical information would be useful. All of these will require substantial changes to the code beyond the capabilities of visualisation with pure D3.js.

Bhāṣācitra is one step of our larger goal of improving the study of South Asian languages with computational methods. Our future work on historical/comparative linguistics (Arora and Farris, 2021) and corpus linguistics for under-studied languages of the region will benefit from Bhāṣācitra's

visualisation capabilities.

7   Conclusion

We developed and presented Bhāṣācitra, a database of linguistic resources for South Asia and a language visualisation system based on location data from those resources. We analysed the coverage of our database and used the areal mapping system to visualise phoneme inventories and Indo-Aryan sound change outcomes. We hope that researchers find the tool useful especially as we move forward with studying the typology of South Asian languages.

Acknowledgments

We thank Kaushalya Perera for providing her personal linguistic bibliography for Sinhala, Erik Anonby for showing us the *Atlas of the Languages of Iran* (ALI) project, and Henrik Liljegren for pointing us to his work on Hindu Kush typology.

We also thank Nathan Schneider for his helpful comments on the paper and Ananya Chakravarti for the useful discussion when devising this project.

References

Muhammad Abdul-Mageed, Hassan Alhuzali, and Mohamed Elaraby. 2018. You tweet what you speak: A city-level dataset of Arabic dialects. In *Proceedings of the Eleventh International Conference on Language Resources and Evaluation (LREC 2018)*, Miyazaki, Japan. European Language Resources Association (ELRA).

Erik Anonby, Mortaza Taheri-Ardali, and Amos Hayes. 2019. The Atlas of the Languages of Iran (ALI): A research overview. *Iranian studies*, 52(1–2):199–230.

Erik Anonby, Mortaza Taheri-Ardali, Fraser Taylor, and Amos Hayes. 2018. Atlas of the Languages of Iran.

Aryaman Arora and Adam Farris. 2021. *Jambu*. Georgetown University, Washington.

Paul Arsenault. 2017. Retroflexion in South Asia: Typological, genetic, and areal patterns. *Journal of South Asian Languages and Linguistics*, 4(1):1–53.

Ronald E Asher. 2008. Language in historical context. *Language in South Asia*, pages 31–48.

Joan L. G. Baart and Esther L. Baart-Bremer. 2001. *Bibliography of languages of northern Pakistan*. NIPS–SIL Working Paper Series. National Institute of Pakistan Studies, Quaid-i-Azam University and Summer Institute of Linguistics.

---

[6]We thank both reviewers for pointing out this limitation.

Elena Bashir. 2016. Contact and convergence. In Hans Henrich Hock and Elena Bashir, editors, *The Languages and Linguistics of South Asia: A Comprehensive Guide*. De Gruyter Mouton.

Michael Bostock, Vadim Ogievetsky, and Jeffrey Heer. 2011. D^3 data-driven documents. *IEEE Transactions on Visualization and Computer Graphics*, 17(12):2301–2309.

Gerd Carling, Filip Larsson, Chundra A. Cathcart, Niklas Johansson, Arthur Holmer, Erich Round, and Rob Verhoeven. 2018. Diachronic Atlas of Comparative Linguistics (DiACL)—a database for ancient language typology. *PLOS ONE*, 13(10):1–20.

Chundra Cathcart. 2019a. Gaussian process models of sound change in Indo-Aryan dialectology. In *Proceedings of the 1st International Workshop on Computational Approaches to Historical Language Change*, pages 254–264, Florence, Italy. Association for Computational Linguistics.

Chundra Cathcart. 2019b. Toward a deep dialectological representation of Indo-Aryan. In *Proceedings of the Sixth Workshop on NLP for Similar Languages, Varieties and Dialects*, pages 110–119, Ann Arbor, Michigan. Association for Computational Linguistics.

Chundra Cathcart. 2020. A probabilistic assessment of the Indo-Aryan Inner–Outer Hypothesis. *Journal of Historical Linguistics*, 10(1):42–86.

Chundra Cathcart and Taraka Rama. 2020. Disentangling dialects: a neural approach to Indo-Aryan historical phonology and subgrouping. In *Proceedings of the 24th Conference on Computational Natural Language Learning*, pages 620–630, Online. Association for Computational Linguistics.

Ashwini Deo. 2018. Dialects in the Indo-Aryan landscape. In Charles Boberg, John Nerbonne, and Dominic Watt, editors, *The Handbook of Dialectology*, pages 535–546. Wiley Online Library.

Matthew S. Dryer and Martin Haspelmath, editors. 2013. *WALS Online*. Max Planck Institute for Evolutionary Anthropology, Leipzig.

David M. Eberhard, Gary F. Simons, and Charles D. Fennig, editors. 2021. *Ethnologue: Languages of the World*, 24th edition. SIL International.

John J. Gumperz. 1958. Dialect differences and social stratification in a North Indian village. *American Anthropologist*, 60(4):668–682.

Harald Hammarström, Robert Forkel, Martin Haspelmath, and Sebastian Bank. 2020. *Glottolog 4.3*. Max Planck Institute for the Science of Human History.

Taylor Jones. 2015. Toward a description of African American Vernacular English dialect regions using "Black Twitter". *American Speech*, 90(4):403–440.

Aikaterini-Lida Kalouli, Rebecca Kehlbeck, Rita Sevastjanova, Katharina Kaiser, Georg A. Kaiser, and Miriam Butt. 2019. ParHistVis: Visualization of parallel multilingual historical data. In *Proceedings of the 1st International Workshop on Computational Approaches to Historical Language Change*, pages 109–114, Florence, Italy. Association for Computational Linguistics.

Daniel Keim, Gennady Andrienko, Jean-Daniel Fekete, Carsten Görg, Jörn Kohlhammer, and Guy Melançon. 2008. Visual analytics: Definition, process, and challenges. In *Information visualization*, pages 154–175. Springer.

William A. Kretzschmar. 2001. Linguistic databases of the American Linguistic Atlas Project (ALAP).

Yasuo Kumagai. 2016. Developing the Linguistic Atlas of Japan Database and advancing analysis of geographical distributions of dialects. In Marie-Hélène Côté, Remco Knooihuizen, and John Nerbonne, editors, *The future of dialects: Selected papers from Methods in Dialectology XV*. Language Science Press.

Henrk Liljegren, Robert Forkel, Nina Knobloch, and Noa Lange. 2021. Hindu Kush areal typology (version v1.0).

Johann-Mattis List, Simon J Greenhill, Tiago Tresoldi, and Robert Forkel. 2019. LingPy. A Python library for quantitative tasks in historical linguistics.

Alan M MacEachren. 2017. Leveraging big (geo) data with (geo) visual analytics: Place as the next frontier. In *Spatial data handling in big data era*, pages 139–155. Springer.

Colin P. Masica. 1993. *The Indo-Aryan languages*. Cambridge Lamguage Surveys. Cambridge University Press, Cambridge.

Steven Moran and Daniel McCloy, editors. 2019. *PHOIBLE 2.0*. Max Planck Institute for the Science of Human History, Jena.

Yugo Murawaki. 2020. Latent geographical factors for analyzing the evolution of dialects in contact. In *Proceedings of the 2020 Conference on Empirical Methods in Natural Language Processing (EMNLP)*, pages 959–976, Online. Association for Computational Linguistics.

Harold Orton, Stewart Sanderson, and John Widdowson, editors. 1998. *The linguistic atlas of England*. Psychology Press.

Kaushalya Perera. 2021. Personal communication.

John Peterson. 2018. Bibliography for seldom studied and endangered South Asian languages.

A. K. Ramanujan and Colin Masica. 2016. *Toward a Phonological Typology of the Indian Linguistic Area*, pages 543–577. De Gruyter Mouton.

N. Ramaswami. 1999. *Common Linguistic Features in Indian Languages: Phonetics.* Central Institute of Indian Languages.

Christopher Shackle. 1980. Hindko in Kohat and Peshawar. *Bulletin of the School of Oriental and African Studies, University of London,* 43(3):482–510.

Ralph Lilley Turner. 1962–1966. *A comparative dictionary of the Indo-Aryan languages.* Oxford University Press.

A Source format

Below is reference metadata for Shackle (1980) in JSON format; note the location annotations and the topic data.

```
{
    "type": "article",
    "title": "Hindko in Kohat and Peshawar",
    "author": ["Christopher Shackle"],
    "journal": "Bulletin of the School...",
    "year": 1980,
    "volume": 43,
    "number": 3,
    "pages": "482--510",
    "url": "https://www.jstor.org/stable/615737",
    "languages": {
        "Hindko": ["Kohat", "Peshawar"]
    },
    "topics": ["overview"]
}
```

Modeling the Evolution of Word Senses
with Force-Directed Layouts of Co-occurrence Networks

Robert Schwanhold[1] and **Tim Repke**[2] and **Ralf Krestel**[2]

Hasso Plattner Insitute

University of Potsdam, Germany

[1] `robert.schwanhold@student.hpi.de`

[2] `fist.lastname@hpi.uni-potsdam.de`

Abstract

Languages evolve over time and the meaning of words can shift. Furthermore, individual words can have multiple senses. However, existing language models often only reflect one word sense per word and do not reflect semantic changes over time. While there are language models that can either model semantic change of words or multiple word senses, none of them cover both aspects simultaneously. We propose a novel force-directed graph layout algorithm to draw a network of frequently co-occurring words. In this way, we are able to use the drawn graph to visualize the evolution of word senses. In addition, we hope that jointly modeling semantic change and multiple senses of words results in improvements for the individual tasks.

1   Introduction

Language is dynamic and constantly evolving which leads to changes in the context in which individual words are used and thereby shifting the meaning of words over time. In addition to this semantic change, novel words are introduced or existing words get additional meanings. On the other hand, certain old word meanings can also disappear from active usage in a language. This results in *multiple word senses* per word which in turn can change or shift their *meaning over time*. Current language models typically do not reflect the dynamic and multi-sense aspect of words. There are approaches which tackle one of the aspects, for example, multiple senses (Reisinger and Mooney, 2010) or semantic change (Hamilton et al., 2016).

Static word embeddings, such as word2vec (Mikolov et al., 2013), can only reflect the prevalent meaning a the word as it appears in the training data. Contextualized word embeddings, such as BERT (Devlin et al., 2019), circumvent this issue by including the surrounding words for each usage of the word. However, by using this approach, the representation of a word has to be computed for each time it appears. Furthermore, these models cannot inherently tell which or even how many different senses a word has or how it changed over time.

The boundary between a new word sense and a shift in meaning is blurred. To illustrate this, consider the term "rock". It has various meanings, e.g., in the context of geology: stone and in the context of music: genre. But those individual meanings are not static. Rock music in the 1960's is a lot different compared to rock in the 1990's, for example. Nevertheless, in this case we would argue that the meaning has evolved — the context of usage has changed, and not that there was a new sense added. The problem naturally decomposes into two parts: identifying a sense for a given word in context and tracking the shift in meaning over time.

In this work, we propose a novel data-driven approach that can reflect multiple senses of words as well as how word senses change by jointly modeling different senses over time. We deliberately refrain from defining the senses of a word to be able to also model subtle nuances of different contexts and word usage. To do so, we define a special force-directed graph layout algorithm to align networks of frequently co-occurring words. By modeling words as nodes and connecting co-occurring words via edges, we create a web of language (Dorogovtsev and Mendes, 2001). The algorithm explicitly models multiple word senses by dividing the input data into time slices and duplicating nodes to accommodate changing co-occurrence frequencies. The resulting network layout allows for easy interaction and can be easily explained and understood. This is in contrast to complex embedding models, which function as a black box and are hard to understand intuitively. With this approach, we model the problems of word sense induction and evolution as

Proceedings of the 2nd International Workshop on Computational Approaches to Historical Language Change 2021, pages 58–63

August 6, 2021. ©2021 Association for Computational Linguistics

a kind of community detection task within a graph. But instead of defining a clustering over the nodes, we propose to visualize the relatedness of words using a force-directed graph layout approach.

2 Related Work

Modeling language as a graph has a long tradition (Dorogovtsev and Mendes, 2001; Mihalcea and Radev, 2011; Cong and Liu, 2014; Nastase et al., 2015). We propose to employ word co-occurrence graphs to jointly solve the problems of multiple senses and diachrony. Accordingly, related work can be split into word sense disambiguation, word sense evolution, and approaches that combine both tasks.

Current state-of-the-art models to represent words make use of embeddings. Contextualized word embeddings, such BERT, account for different word senses by computing individual vectors for a word based on its context. Classical, static word embeddings, such as word2vec, use a single vector to represent an individual word. This is problematic because they fail to capture polysemy. Reisinger and Mooney (2010) presented a multi-prototype vector-space model (VSM). The meaning of a word is represented as a set of sense specific vectors. Based on that, Huang et al. (2012) developed a neural network architecture that learns multiple word embeddings per word. However, both of these approaches use a fixed number of clusters, even though different words might have a different number of senses. Brody and Lapata (2009) use a model based on latent Dirichlet allocation (LDA) to solve the word sense induction (WSI) problem. While this approach uses a fixed number of senses across all words, Lau et al. (2012) combine LDA with a varying number of senses per word. However, this approach requires prior knowledge of the number of senses per word. Hierarchical Dirichlet process (HDP), an extension of LDA, can learn the number of topics (or senses in this case) from the data automatically.

Besides the work on detecting word senses, there is also a plethora of work on diachronic modeling of word senses. Kim et al. (2014) separated a text corpus into multiple time slices and trained a model on each time slice to get different word embedding models over time. Diachronic word embeddings were investigated by aligning embeddings trained on consecutive time slices (Hamilton et al., 2016). Bamler and Mandt (2017) developed the concept of *dynamic* word embeddings. Each document has a timestamp. This allows the word embeddings to change over time. Unlike previous approaches, a single model is used to derive the shifts of word embeddings over time. One advantage of such an approach is that the complete training data can be used for one single model. While these papers focus on shifts of words over time, they do not discover if a word has multiple senses. Spitz and Gertz (2018) use a network to model the co-occurrence of terms in documents. Terms that are co-occurring together are connected by an edge. Topics are discovered by finding edges of frequently co-occurring terms. For each document, the publication time is stored which allows filtering the results by a given time span. Gad et al. (2015) use a layout with multiple vertical line segments to visualize the trends of topics over time. Each vertical line segment corresponds to a time slice. For each time slice, the topic distribution is calculated. Common terms of the underlying topics are grouped together and plotted on the vertical line segments. This visualization shows how different topics split up or converge over time. Very recently, SemEval-2020 (Schlechtweg et al., 2020) featured a task for unsupervised lexical semantic change detection, which has led to a plethora of diachronic approaches.

Mitra et al. (2014) use co-occurrence networks to find changes in word senses over time. They distinguish between four different types of the evolution of language senses: the birth of new sense; splits of a sense; joins of senses; death of senses. Candidate nodes for splits are computed with a distributed thesaurus. For each candidate node, a clustering algorithm is run on the neighborhood graph. Each cluster represents a sense of the term associated with the candidate node. As shown by Ehmüller et al. (2020) however, matching clusters across more than two or three time slices causes problems such as sense shifting when matching partially overlapping clusters. Hu et al. (2019) use deep contextualized embeddings to track the senses of words over time. For each word, the distribution of the senses is calculated on a temporal slice of the corpus. Over time, these distributions show which senses gain or loose importance. While this approach tracks the senses over time, it does not discover them. Instead, the senses are extracted from the Oxford dictionary.

3 Force-Direct Graph Layout Algorithm

In this section we describe our force-directed graph layout algorithm for a network of co-occurring words. In this network, each node corresponds to a word in the vocabulary. We first split the corpus in to disjunct sets of documents based on their publication date to create partial corpora across time. For each set, we compute a network of frequently co-occurring words, where the weighted edges represent the frequency of how often words appear in the same context. In our preliminary experiments, we saw promising results by limiting the vocabulary to nouns and using sentences as context windows. In future work, we intend to compare the raw co-occurrence frequencies to more sophisticated measures, such as pointwise mutual information (PMI). We call the sub-networks for individual time periods *period graphs* and edges within each period graph *intra-edges*. We connect nodes representing identical words in neighboring period graphs with *inter-edges*. All edges are undirected.

Force-Directed Layout. Our layout algorithm is inspired by traditional force-directed algorithms. Attractive and repulsive forces are applied on nodes based on their edges and on their proximity to other nodes on a two-dimensional canvas. During the layout process, the positions are iteratively updated to minimize the aggregated forces. Traditionally, nodes are allowed to move freely in both dimensions.

We restrict this layout as follows. We assign each period graph to equidistant vertically aligned parallel axes, which are ordered from left to right according to their time period. Nodes of each period graph are only allowed to move along their respective axis similar to arc diagrams (Saaty, 1964). All other concepts of traditional force-directed layout algorithms remain the same. As two nodes connected by an intra-edge move further apart on the axis of their respective layer graph, the attractive force grows. Repulsive forces between nodes prevent that all nodes are clustered together. Additionally, we introduce another force to reduce the angle of inter-edges.

Figure 1 illustrates a period graph. Initially, nodes are placed randomly along the axis. As a result, some of the edge span long distances. The positions are then iteratively updated until they converge. As shown in Figure 1b, connected compo-

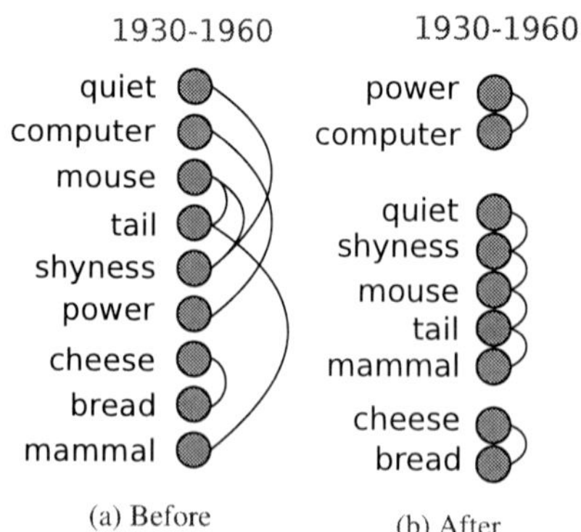

Figure 1: Hand-crafted example of a period graph on initialization and after running our layout algorithm.

nents are clearly separated and all edge lengths are minimal.

Formally, we define the forces between nodes as follows. Let V_t be the set of nodes of the period graph for time slice t and P_v the position along the vertical axis for node v. The updated position of each node in each period graph in an iteration is defined as

$$P_v := P_v + \psi\Big(\alpha F_{intra} + (1 - \alpha)F_{inter} - F_r\Big)$$

where ψ is the learning rate and F_{intra}, F_{inter} and F_r are the forces between nodes in the current layout. We add α to balance the attractive forces within and between different period graphs. The forces acting on node v are defined as

$$F_{intra} := \sum_{u \in N_t(v)} k \times w(\{u, v\}) \times (P_u - P_v)^2.$$

where $w(\{u, v\})$ is the edge weight and $N_t(v)$ is the set of nodes directly connected to v in the current period graph and $N_{t+1}(v)$ is the set of neighbor nodes of v from the next period graph. Corresponding nodes in different period graphs are vertically aligned by

$$F_{inter} := \sum_{v' \in N_{t-1}(v) \cup N_{t+1}(v)} \frac{k}{(P_{v'} - P_v)^2}.$$

We use k as a parameter to control the overall strength of the forces in our system. In physics, this k is a proportionality constant called *Coulomb's constant* (Gerthsen, 2006). The value of k is proportional to the electric permittivity of the charged particles in a vacuum. As in other force-directed

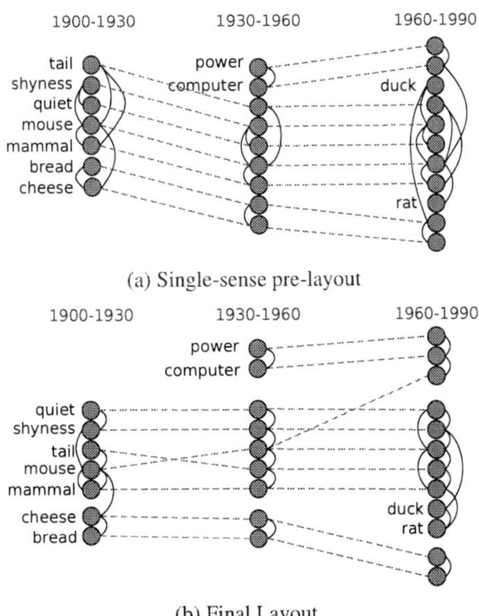

(a) Single-sense pre-layout

(b) Final Layout

Figure 2: Hand-crafted example to illustrate a resulting layout over three time slices of our proposed approach.

graph layout algorithms, we use a repulsive force to prevent overlapping nodes:

$$F_r := \sum_{u \in V_t} \frac{k}{(P_u - P_v)^2}$$

We limit the calculation of repulsive forces between all pairs of nodes to nodes from the same period graph.

Representing Multiple Meanings. Thus far, we described a layout for a graph based on a fixed vocabulary with only one meaning for each word. To reflect multiple senses of a word, we allow the addition of duplicate nodes in a period graph. During the iterative updates of the graph layout, words with multiple senses will cause significantly more stress in the force-directed layout than others. This is due to the fact, that they are associated with different domains, which are likely located far from one another.

We use this to our advantage to discover ambiguous words. First, we run the layout algorithm as described above until it converges. We call the resulting layout our initial layout. In force-based graph drawing algorithms, some nodes induce higher forces on connected or surrounding nodes, causing significant stress in the graph. We identify such nodes duplicate them when the forces of the connecting edges exceed a certain threshold,

which will be determined experimentally. Let node v be such an ambiguous word, then we split it into two nodes v' and v''. The intra-edges that were previously incident to v are replaced by

$$\forall \hat{v} \in N_t(v) : \begin{cases} (\hat{v}, v'), & \text{if } P_{\hat{v}} > P_v \\ (\hat{v}, v''), & otherwise. \end{cases}$$

Afterwards, we add inter-edges to connect v' and v'' to their respective nodes in the previous and following period graphs. This splitting operation can be repeated for the same word again to reflect more than two meanings.

Figure 2 shows an example of the layout before and after adjustment for multiple meanings of words and balancing the forces. Over time, the vocabulary expands and a new meaning of the word "mouse" appears in the context of computers. Note, that in the early days of computing, mice were not used as input devices yet, thus the new sense surfaces only in the last time slice.

4   Evaluation Plan

Word sense detection is hard to evaluate given the lack of annotated ground truth data (Usama et al., 2019). General thesauri could be used but only for the period graph for the latest time slice. To our knowledge, there are no established datasets to evaluate both, the multi-sense aspect of a model, as well as the dynamic evolution of senses. Thus, it is necessary to evaluate our approach with respect to both aspects individually and compare results to respective state-of-the-art approaches.

Evaluation of Word Similarities. Even though our proposed algorithm focuses on word sense detection, the underlying co-occurrence network can as well be used for other analysis tasks, e.g., word similarity. The vicinity of nodes in a period graph should roughly compare to the neighborhood of vectors in word embeddings trained or fine-tuned on the same set of documents of one time slice.

Evaluation of the Number of Senses. The Merriam-Webster dictionary stores metadata for its entries, e.g., a section "First Known Use of ...", which lists the year where a sense of that word was first used. Unfortunately, this information does not exist for all entries. However, we can use the existing ones to estimate how well our model performs in finding senses for a specific time period. In addition, manually created thesauri, such as Word-Net (Miller, 1995), can also be used.

Contextualized Word Representations State-of-the-art embedding models, such as BERT, compute the representation of a word based on the context it appears in. A competitive baseline could be based on contextual word embeddings. Using a pre-trained model, we apply it to each appearance of a word in a corpus. Each meaning of a word should form a cluster of contextual embedding vectors. By doing this for every time slice, we can compare the number of clusters and their similarity neighborhoods to the layout of our graph.

Qualitative Evaluation of Selected Word Sense Changes. In a collaboration with digital humanities experts, we developed a use case for a qualitative evaluation by analyzing the different contexts of mentions of natural phenomena in German fiction novels. This allows to qualitatively compare selected parts of our layout to expected changes discussed in relevant literature on digital eco-criticism.

5   Conclusion

In this paper, we proposed a novel approach for a multi-sense time-sensitive word similarity model. As it is based on a force-directed graph layout of aligned co-occurrence networks, it allows direct and intuitive interpretation as opposed to most black box embedding models. In future work, we are developing the model further and plan to perform an extensive evaluation as discussed in Section 4. To this end, we will compare our model to existing state-of-the-art language models for word sense disambiguation and evolution, as well as to community detection methods working on graphs.

References

Robert Bamler and Stephan Mandt. 2017. Dynamic word embeddings. In *Proceedings of the International Conference on Machine Learning (ICML)*, volume 70 of *Proceedings of Machine Learning Research*, pages 380–389. JMLR Inc. and Microtome Publishing.

Samuel Brody and Mirella Lapata. 2009. Bayesian word sense induction. In *Proceedings of the Conference of the European Chapter of the Association for Computational Linguistics (EACL)*, pages 103–111. Association for Computational Linguistics.

Jin Cong and Haitao Liu. 2014. Approaching human language with complex networks. *Physics of Life Reviews*, 11(4):598–618.

Jacob Devlin, Ming-Wei Chang, Kenton Lee, and Kristina Toutanova. 2019. BERT: Pre-training of deep bidirectional transformers for language understanding. In *Proceedings of the Annual Conference of the North American Chapter of the Association for Computational Linguistics (NAACL)*, pages 4171–4186. Association for Computational Linguistics.

Sergey N Dorogovtsev and José Fernando F Mendes. 2001. Language as an evolving word web. *Proceedings of the Royal Society of London. Series B: Biological Sciences*, 268(1485):2603–2606.

Jan Ehmüller, Lasse Kohlmeyer, Holly McKee, Daniel Paeschke, Tim Repke, Ralf Krestel, and Felix Naumann. 2020. Sense tree: Discovery of new word senses with graph-based scoring. In *Proceedings of the Conference "Lernen, Wissen, Daten, Analysen" (LWDA)*, volume 2738 of *CEUR Workshop Proceedings*, pages 246–257. CEUR-WS.org.

Samah Gad, Waqas Javed, Sohaib Ghani, Niklas Elmqvist, E. Thomas Ewing, Keith N. Hampton, and Naren Ramakrishnan. 2015. Themedelta: Dynamic segmentations over temporal topic models. *IEEE Transactions on Visualization and Computer Graphics (TVCG)*, 21(5):672–685.

Christian Gerthsen. 2006. *Gerthsen Physik*. Springer-Verlag.

William L Hamilton, Jure Leskovec, and Dan Jurafsky. 2016. Diachronic word embeddings reveal statistical laws of semantic change. In *Proceedings of the Annual Meeting of the Association for Computational Linguistics (ACL)*, pages 1489–1501. Association for Computational Linguistics.

Renfen Hu, Shen Li, and Shichen Liang. 2019. Diachronic sense modeling with deep contextualized word embeddings: An ecological view. In *Proceedings of the Annual Meeting of the Association for Computational Linguistics (ACL)*, pages 3899–3908. Association for Computational Linguistics.

Eric H. Huang, Richard Socher, Christopher D. Manning, and Andrew Y. Ng. 2012. Improving word representations via global context and multiple word prototypes. In *Proceedings of the Annual Meeting of the Association for Computational Linguistics (ACL)*, pages 873–882. Association for Computational Linguistics.

Yoon Kim, Yi-I Chiu, Kentaro Hanaki, Darshan Hegde, and Slav Petrov. 2014. Temporal analysis of language through neural language models. In *Proceedings of the Workshop on Language Technologies and Computational Social Science@ACL*, pages 61–65. Association for Computational Linguistics.

Jey Han Lau, Paul Cook, Diana McCarthy, David Newman, and Timothy Baldwin. 2012. Word sense induction for novel sense detection. In *Proceedings of the Conference of the European Chapter of the Association for Computational Linguistics (EACL)*, pages 591–601. Association for Computational Linguistics.

Rada Mihalcea and Dragomir Radev. 2011. *Graph-based natural language processing and information retrieval*. Cambridge University Press.

Tomás Mikolov, Ilya Sutskever, Kai Chen, Gregory S. Corrado, and Jeffrey Dean. 2013. Distributed representations of words and phrases and their compositionality. In *Proceedings of the Conference on Neural Information Processing Systems (NIPS)*, pages 3111–3119.

George A. Miller. 1995. Wordnet: A lexical database for english. *Communications of the ACM*, 38(11):39–41.

Sunny Mitra, Ritwik Mitra, Martin Riedl, Chris Biemann, Animesh Mukherjee, and Pawan Goyal. 2014. That's sick dude!: Automatic identification of word sense change across different timescales. In *Proceedings of the Annual Meeting of the Association for Computational Linguistics (ACL)*, pages 1020–1029. Association for Computational Linguistics.

Vivi Nastase, Rada Mihalcea, and Dragomir R Radev. 2015. A survey of graphs in natural language processing. *Natural Language Engineering*, 21(5):665–698.

Joseph Reisinger and Raymond J. Mooney. 2010. Multi-prototype vector-space models of word meaning. In *Proceedings of the Annual Conference of the North American Chapter of the Association for Computational Linguistics (NAACL)*, pages 109–117. Association for Computational Linguistics.

Thomas L Saaty. 1964. The minimum number of intersections in complete graphs. *Proceedings of the National Academy of Sciences of the United States of America*, 52(3):688.

Dominik Schlechtweg, Barbara McGillivray, Simon Hengchen, Haim Dubossarsky, and Nina Tahmasebi. 2020. Semeval-2020 task 1: Unsupervised lexical semantic change detection. In *Proceedings of the Workshop on Semantic Evaluation*, pages 1–23.

Andreas Spitz and Michael Gertz. 2018. Entity-centric topic extraction and exploration: A network-based approach. In *Proceedings of the European Conference on Information Retrieval (ECIR)*, volume 10772 of *Lecture Notes in Computer Science*, pages 3–15. Springer.

Muhammad Usama, Junaid Qadir, Aunn Raza, Hunain Arif, Kok-Lim Alvin Yau, Yehia Elkhatib, Amir Hussain, and Ala I. Al-Fuqaha. 2019. Unsupervised machine learning for networking: Techniques, applications and research challenges. *IEEE Access*, 7:65579–65615.

Tracking Semantic Change in Cognate Sets for English and Romance Languages

Ana Sabina Uban♠,♡,◇ Alina Maria Cristea♡ Anca Dinu♣,♡
Liviu P. Dinu♠,♡ Simona Georgescu♣,♡ Laurențiu Zoicaș ♣,♡

♡Human Languages Technologies Research Center, University of Bucharest
♠ Faculty of Mathematics and Computer Science, University of Bucharest
♣Faculty of Foreign Languages and Literatures, University of Bucharest
◇PRHLT Research Center, Universitat Politècnica de València

ana.uban+acad@gmail.com, alina.cristea@fmi.unibuc.ro, anca.dinu@lls.unibuc.ro
ldinu@fmi.unibuc.ro, simona.georgescu@lls.unibuc.ro, laurentiu.zoicas@lls.unibuc.ro

Abstract

Semantic divergence in related languages is a key concern of historical linguistics. We cross-linguistically investigate the semantic divergence of cognate pairs in English and Romance languages, by means of word embeddings. To this end, we introduce a new curated dataset of cognates in all pairs of those languages. We describe the types of errors that occurred during the automated cognate identification process and manually correct them. Additionally, we label the English cognates according to their etymology, separating them into two groups: old borrowings and recent borrowings. On this curated dataset, we analyse word properties such as frequency and polysemy, and the distribution of similarity scores between cognate sets in different languages. We automatically identify different clusters of English cognates, setting a new direction of research in cognates, borrowings and possibly false friends analysis in related languages.

1 Introduction and Related Work

Semantic change – that is, change in the meaning of individual words (Campbell, 1998) – is a continuous, inevitable process stemming from numerous reasons and influenced by various factors, most of which anchored in the speakers' experiences, encyclopedic knowledge and cognitive mechanisms (Rousseau, 2000). Words are continuously changing, with new senses emerging all the time. Campbell (1998) presents 11 types of semantic change, that are generally classified in two wide categories: narrowing and widening.

In recent years, multiple computational linguistic studies have focused on the issue of semantic change, tracking the shift in the meaning of words by looking at their usage across time in corpora dating from different time periods. More than this, computational linguists have also tried to systematically analyse the principles and statistical laws governing semantic change, such as the law of parallel change and the law of differentiation (Xu and Kemp, 2015), the law of conformity and the law of innovation (Hamilton et al., 2016), or the law of prototypicality (Dubossarsky et al., 2015). More recently, Dubossarsky et al. (2017) revisited some of the semantic change laws proposed in previous literature, claiming that a more rigorous consideration of control conditions when modelling these laws leads to the conclusion that they are weaker or less reliable than reported. More extensive surveys of computational studies relating to semantic change have been conducted by Kutuzov et al. (2018) and Tahmasebi et al. (2018).

Most previous computational studies on lexical-semantic change have looked at the semantic change of the words within one language, treating each language separately. However, words do not evolve only in their own language in isolation, but are rather inherited and borrowed between and across languages.

In most cases, cognates have preserved similar meanings across languages, but there are also exceptions. These are called deceptive cognates or, more commonly, *false friends*. Here we use the definition of cognates that refers to words with similar appearance and some common etymology and use *true cognates* to refer to cognates which also have a common meaning (e.g. Ro. *mână*, It. *mano*, Fr. *main*, Es. *mano*, Pt. *mão* 'hand'), and *deceptive cognates* or *false friends* to refer to cognate pairs which do not have the same meaning (anymore) (e.g. Ro. *pleca* 'to leave' / Fr. *plier* 'to fold' / Es. *llegar* 'to arrive', all of them originated from Lat. *plicare* 'to fold').

Most linguists found psychological and structural factors to be the main cause of semantic change (Meillet, 1906; Coseriu, 1958), but the evolution of technology and socio-cultural changes are not to be omitted. Moreover, when

64

Proceedings of the 2nd International Workshop on Computational Approaches to Historical Language Change 2021, pages 64–74
August 6, 2021. ©2021 Association for Computational Linguistics

a word enters a new language, features specific to that particular language can affect the way it is used and contribute to shaping its meaning through time: existing words in the same language, as well as socio-linguistic, cultural and historical factors (for details concerning the semantic fields most permeable to borrowing, in accordance with the socio-cultural circumstances, cf. Tadmor (2009)). The evolution of cognate words in different languages can be seen as a collection of different parallel histories of the proto-word from entering the new languages to its current state. Based on this view, we rely on a different framework for studying semantic change: instead of comparing *monolingual* texts from *different time periods* as ways to track meanings of words at different stages in time – we compare *present meanings* of cognate words across *different languages*, viewing them as snapshots in time of each of the word's different histories of evolution.

A comprehensive list of cognates and false friends for every language pair is difficult to find or manually build – this is why applications often rely on automatically identifying them. Related to our task, there have been a number of previous studies attempting to automatically extract pairs of true cognates and false friends. Most methods are based either on orthographic and phonetic similarity or require large parallel corpora or dictionaries (Inkpen et al., 2005; Nakov et al., 2009; Chen and Skiena, 2016; St Arnaud et al., 2017). There have been few previous studies using word embeddings for the detection of false friends or cognates, usually using simple methods on only one or two pairs of languages (Torres and Aluísio, 2011; Castro et al., 2018).

Uban et al. (2019a) propose a method for identifying and correcting false friends, as well as define a measure of their "falseness", using cross-lingual word embeddings and automatically extracted cognate sets (Uban et al., 2019b; Uban and Dinu, 2020; Uban et al., 2021). Expanding upon the direction proposed there, we create a new curated dataset of cognate sets in English and Romance languages. Additionally, we label the cognate sets according to their etymology and the period they entered the language, separating them into two distinct groups: *old borrowings* and *recent borrowings*. On this dataset, we investigate patterns related to the distribution of frequency, polysemy and cross-lingual semantic sim-

ilarity across cognates, and show that the similarity distributions of English words show a specific bimodal pattern. We provide qualitative analyses and extensive linguistic interpretations for all our findings.

We bring several contributions to the computational study of semantic change and cognate words. To the best of our knowledge, we are the first to approach the problem of dating cognates based on their semantic content. Analysing the formal properties of cognates (i.e. their word form) is a method that is well-known in computational historical linguistics to gauge how language families have evolved (Ciobanu and Dinu, 2015). Computational approaches to analyse changes in meanings of cognate sets in order to investigate language contact settings have not been considered in historical computational linguistics research. Additionally, we publish a novel electronically readable dataset with high quality annotations regarding the period a word entered the English language, for a selection of cognates in English and Romance languages. To our knowledge, it is the first of its kind, and we hope it can help further research into computer-assisted analysis of cognate words.

1.1 Preliminaries

Cognates are words in sister languages (languages descending from a common ancestor) with a common proto-word. For example, the Spanish word *paz* and the French word *paix* are cognates, as they both descend from the Latin word *pacem* (N. *pax*, meaning *peace*) – see Figure 1.

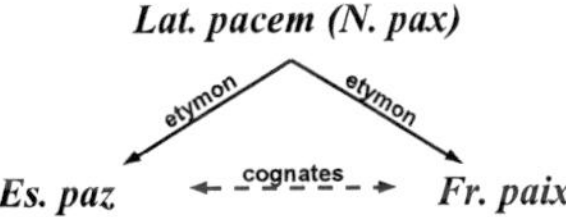

Figure 1: Example of cognates and their common ancestor: *peace*.

An important distinction is to be made between inherited words and borrowings: we speak of *inherited words* when referring to those lexemes that have been preserved from the ancestor language in the vernacular languages by uninterrupted oral usage, thus taking part in the process of language formation; by *borrowing* (also known as *loanword*), on the contrary, we understand any word that has been adopted in a language *A* from a language *B* after the language *A* has passed through its basic formation period (Reinheimer Ripeanu, 2001, 2004). According to Hall (1960), there is no such thing as a "pure language" – a language "without any borrowing from a foreign language". The process in which words enter one language from another is called *linguistic borrowing*. The average borrowing rate, reaching 24.2% (Tadmor, 2009), turns the borrowing process into one of the main resorts of lexical enrichment. The result of the borrowing process depends on numerous factors, such as the length and intensity of the contact and the extent to which the populations in question are bilingual (Campbell, 1998). Although admittedly regarded as relevant factors in the history of a language (McMahon et al., 2005), borrowings bias the genetic classification of the languages, characterizing them as being closer than they actually are (Minett and Wang, 2003). Thus, the need for discriminating between cognates and borrowings emerged (Ciobanu and Dinu, 2019). Heggarty (2012) acknowledged the necessity and difficulty of the task, emphasizing the role of the "computerized approaches" (Ciobanu and Dinu, 2015; Tsvetkov et al., 2015).

The concept of "Latin inherited word" can only be applied to the Romance languages, as these are the only languages whose ancestor is Latin. The descendants of the same Latin word in various (if not all) Romance languages are called "cognates" (ex. Ro. *drept* "right", It. *dritto*, Fr. *droit*, Es. *derecho*, Pt. *direito* are cognates, as they are all inherited from Lat. *directus*). On the other hand, the Romance languages have also experimented a period of "relatinization" (starting as early as the 13th century in Western Europe), when they massively borrowed words, through a cultural, written channel, from the same language from which they originate: in this case, Latin does not play the role of ancestor language any more, but it represents a non-contemporary source of lexical enrichment (Reinheimer Ripeanu, 2004). To give an example, the same Latin word *directus* has been borrowed in Ro. *direct* "direct", It. *diretto*, Fr. *direct*, Es. *directo*, Pt. *directo*, in a period that varies from the 13th century for French, to the 19th century for Romanian.

In order to maintain the distinction between the two possible channels (oral vs written) through which Latin words entered the Romance lexica (inherited word vs borrowing), and at the same time to highlight the genetic relation between the Romance lexemes in either case, we have adopted a twofold terminology: we shall use the concept of *real cognate* to refer to the relationship between inherited words that come from a common ancestor (Ro. *drept* "right", It. *dritto*, Fr. *droit*, Es. *derecho*, Pt. *direito*), and *virtual cognate* to denote the connection between words that have been borrowed from the same Latin etymon (Ro. *direct* "direct", It. *diretto*, Fr. *direct*, Es. *directo*, Pt. *directo*).

When it comes to English, we can only use the term "borrowing" whenever we refer to a word of Latin origin. Given that the accuracy of our dataset analysis involves a clear distinction between the two main historical stages when clusters of words of Latin origin were integrated in the English lexicon, we established an internal differentiation between *"old borrowings"* (that penetrated English through Old French, that means anytime before the first half of the 15th century) and *"recent borrowings"* (taken directly from Latin, from the second half of the 15th century to the present day).

It is easily understandable that the Latin lexical thesaurus has offered to the English language more or less the same lexical items that it disseminated in the Romance languages (either by inheritance or by cultural transmission). In this case, the English borrowing will equally be considered a *"virtual cognate"* of the Romance lexical items coming from the same Latin etymon, regardless if these are inherited or borrowed (e.g. En. *direct* vs Ro. *drept/direct*, It. *dritto/diretto*, Fr. *droit/direct*, Es. *derecho/directo*, Pt. *direito/directo*).

2   Cognates Dataset

As our data source, we use the list of cognate sets in Romance languages proposed by Ciobanu and Dinu (2014). It contains 3,218 complete cognate sets in Romanian, French, Italian, Spanish and Portuguese, along with their Latin common ancestors, extracted from online etymology dictionaries. The dictionary-based approach for identifying cognates, described in detail in (Ciobanu and Dinu, 2013), comprises two steps: firstly, the etymological information is extracted from electronic dictionaries; secondly, the etymologies are matched: words with the same language of origin and the same etymon are considered to be cognates. This approach answers the question raised by Swadesh (1954): "Given a small collection of likely-looking cognates, how can one

Romanian	French	Italian	Spanish	Portuguese	English	Latin ancestor
arhitect	architecte	architetto	arquitecto	arquiteto	architect	architectus

Table 1: Example of a cognate set: *architect*.

definitely determine whether they are really the residue of common origin and not the workings of pure chance or some other factor?", as the analysis is performed only on words that share a common etymology. We augment the dataset with the corresponding cognate in English (in the broad sense, since these are borrowings) for a subset of 305 of these cognate sets, using the same approach that was used for building the original dataset.[1] Considering a Romance cognate set and an English cognate candidate, both with Latin etymology, we compare their etymons. If they match, we identify the English word as being part of the cognate set. One complete example of a cognate set in Romance languages and English for the word *architect* is represented in Table 1.

We curate the obtained cognate sets and include high-quality annotations separating them into two groups according to their etymology (*old borrowings* and *recent borrowings*), provided by experts in linguistics. Out of the total 305 cognate pairs, we find 105 old borrowings and 135 recent borrowings (while the rest cannot be assigned a clear label or represent errors). We provide more details on data curation and evaluation in the following section.

2.1 Dataset Evaluation and Manual Curation

Our approach needs not be totally automated, nor completely manual, but rather computer-assisted.

The corpus was built by extracting the basic information from electronic dictionaries of Romance languages, as described in detail in (Ciobanu and Dinu, 2014), as well as the *Collins Dictionary*[2] for English, followed by a detailed curation of the lexical sets obtained, with the aid of the following dictionaries:

- for English: *Online Etymology Dictionary*[3]; *The Oxford Dictionary of English Etymology* (Onions et al., 1994); *Merriam-Webster*[4];
- for Romanian: *Dicţionar Explicativ Român* (DEX[5]), *Dicţionarul Etimologic al Limbii Române* (Ciorănescu, 2002)[6];
- for Italian: *Il Nuovo De Mauro*[7];
- for French: *Trésor de la Langue Française Informatisé*[8], *Dictionnaire historique de la langue française* (Rey, 2011); *Le Grand Robert* (CD);
- for Spanish: *Diccionario de Uso del Español* (Moliner, 2007); *Diccionario de la Lengua Española*[9];
- for Portuguese: *Dicionario Priberam*[10].

The annotations made by the expert linguists for the English cognates had to give account of the following data: on the one hand, the way they entered the English language (either as direct borrowings from Latin or via French), and, on the other hand, the period when they were first attested (before the first half of the 15th century or after). By using these two criteria, we could decide whether a cognate is an old or recent borrowing.

To evaluate our dataset, we consider a cognate set to be correct if all cognates in the set were correctly identified for each language. We evaluate not only the automatic extraction, but also the etymological information from the electronic dictionaries. We ought to mention that we classified as an error any type of distancing from the standard version we were expecting (e.g. a conjugated form of the verb instead of its infinitive, for instance *admits* instead of *admit*, or, when it comes to Romance languages, the feminine form of a noun or adjective instead of the standard masculine variant). Thus, the resulted overall accuracy was 53% (161 correctly identified cognate sets out of the 305 automatically extracted ones). The overall accuracy represents the percentage of cognate sets in which the comprising cognates are correct for

---

[1]The dataset size was reduced when including English mainly because of two reasons: 1) we did not identify etymologies for all English cognate candidates; 2) some cognate sets from the initial dataset might not have a corresponding cognate in English.

[2]https://www.collinsdictionary.com/

[3]https://etymonline.com/

[4]https://www.merriam-webster.com/

[5]https://dexonline.ro/

[6]cf. https://dexonline.ro/

[7]https://dizionario.internazionale.it/

[8]http://atilf.atilf.fr/

[9]https://dle.rae.es/

[10]https://dicionario.priberam.org/

all languages. In other words, if at least one cognate was incorrect, we considered the cognate set to be incorrectly identified. Per language, we obtained the following accuracy values: 70.8% (English), 82.6% (Spanish), 77.3% (French), 80.0% (Italian), 79.6% (Portuguese), 81.3% (Romanian). In this case, we computed accuracy individually for each language, without looking at the entire cognate sets. As expected, the accuracy values per language were higher than the accuracy per cognate sets. We have also computed the average normalized edit distance (Levenshtein, 1965) between the correct cognates and those extracted automatically, as a way to assess the degree of minor errors in word forms as opposed to entirely incorrect cognate associations, obtaining the following values: 0.20 (English), 0.14 (Spanish), 0.17 (French), 0.14 (Italian), 0.16 (Portuguese), 0.14 (Romanian). Thus, to obtain an accurate dataset, a second stage of manual curation and error removal was necessary. We observed several types of errors that generally occur due to the interference between similar forms, which the machine cannot discriminate, but also due to lack of information in the source of the data (dictionaries). Most of those errors consisted in a missing cognate or an incorrect one, while some were incorrect associations of words that had no common etymology. Particularly, a common type of error is the selection of different grammatical categories from one language to another (En. *cause* – that can be either verb or noun – is placed next to Es. *causar* – verb –, but It. *causa*, Ro. *cauza* – noun).

Another inaccuracy – not fully mistaken and at the same time very interesting from an etymological point of view – is the identification of an English lexical item that only has a distant etymological connection to the Romance words selected as its cognates: for instance, next to Es. *fuego* "fire", It. *fuoco*, Fr. *feu*, etc. – all inherited from Lat. *focus* –, the machine placed En. *fuel*, that, although not directly derived from Lat. *focus*, was borrowed from the Old French descendant of a derivative of *focus*, namely *focale* (Fr. *fouaille*). Another case of placing at the same level different strata of virtual cognates is that of En. *brave* (borrowed from It. or Es. *bravo*, at their turn inherited from Lat. *barbarus* "barbarian") that appeared next to the loanwords It. *barbaro* "barbarian", Es. *bárbaro*, etc. Intrinsically related to this inaccuracy was the lack of dating of the exact period when the words entered a language. As a particular observation, we found that the errors generated by the automatic processing sometimes coincide with the cases where speakers themselves misinterpret the origin of a word (a linguistic process known as "folk etymology" or "paretymology", i.e. the false connection between two similar words that etymologically have nothing in common, leading to a change of one of them either in form or in meaning (Schweickard, 2008)).

We report the results on the curated dataset, which we make available publicly[11].

3 Measuring Cognate Divergence

3.1 Methods

Word embeddings have become a standard method for measuring lexical semantic similarity in the field of computational analysis of semantic change.

In our study, we make use of word embeddings computed using the FastText algorithm, pre-trained on Wikipedia for the six languages in question. The vectors have 300 dimensions and were obtained using the skip-gram model described by Bojanowski et al. (2016) with default parameters. In our cross-lingual setup, we make use of cross-lingual word embeddings in order to compute semantic similarities between words in different languages. Obtaining cross-lingual word embeddings entails training word embedding spaces for each language separately, then applying an alignment algorithm across the obtained vector spaces in order to create a common space.

This is accomplished through an alignment algorithm, which consists of finding a linear transformation between the two spaces, that on average optimally transforms each vector in one embedding space into a vector in the second embedding space, minimizing the distance between a few seed word pairs (for which it is known that they have the same meaning), based on a small bilingual dictionary. For our purposes, we use the publicly available multilingual alignment matrices that were published by Smith et al. (2017). Finally, we compute semantic similarities for each pair of cognate words using the cosine similarity between their corresponding vectors in the shared embedding space.

We separately extract word frequency scores for all words in the dataset. For measuring fre-

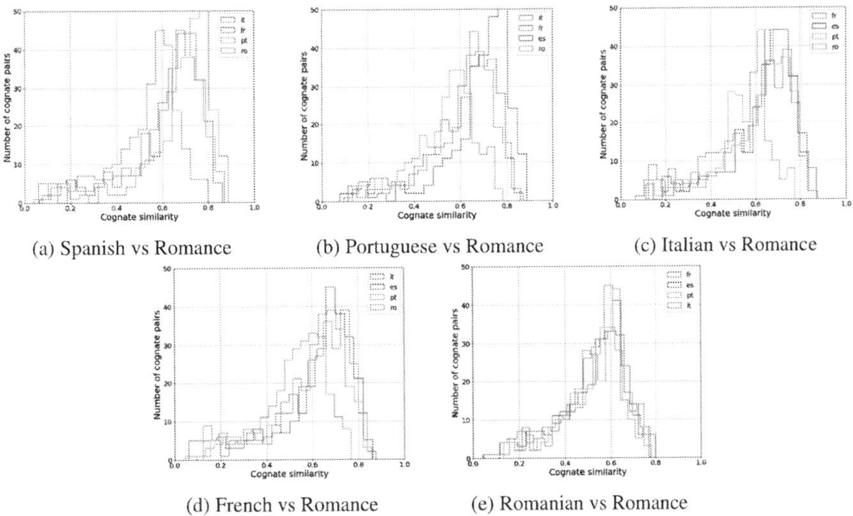

(a) Spanish vs Romance   (b) Portuguese vs Romance   (c) Italian vs Romance

(d) French vs Romance   (e) Romanian vs Romance

Figure 2: Distributions of cross-lingual similarity scores between cognates.

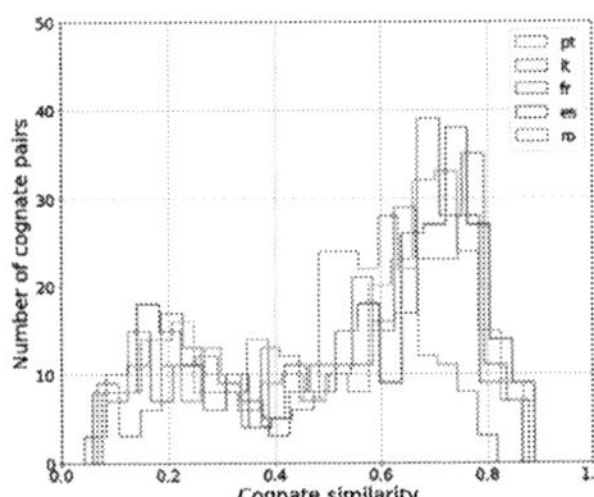

Figure 3: Distribution of similarities for automatically extracted English cognate sets according to the proposed algorithm.

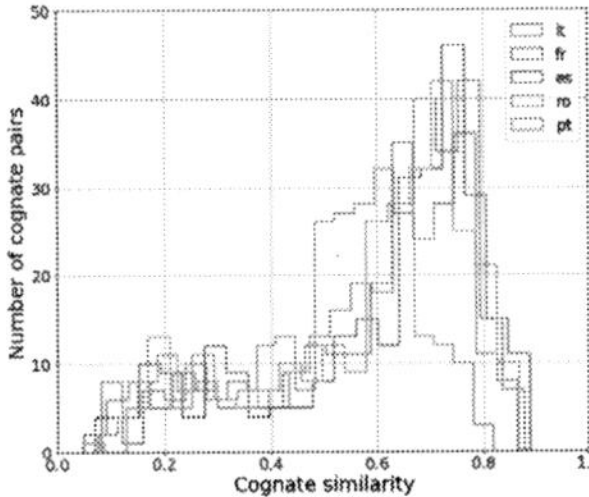

Figure 4: Distribution of similarities for curated English cognate sets according to the proposed algorithm.

quency, we use the multilingual Wordfreq Python library (Speer et al., 2018), which estimates word frequency based on multiple corpora (such as Wikipedia and Twitter). For most of the languages we consider, we are able to extract frequency scores for the majority of words in our cognate sets, with a coverage of at least 92% of the words in our cognate sets for every language considered, except for Romanian, which has a poorer coverage of only 60%. The library provides a log-

normalized frequency score, ranging between 0 and 10 on a logarithmic scale, with higher scores corresponding to more frequent words.

We additionally measure word polysemy, making use of Open Multilingual WordNet (OMW) (Bond and Paik, 2012). In this way, the polysemy of a word can be defined as the number of synsets that it is part of in WordNet. We have to exclude Romanian from this analysis, since it is not supported in OMW.

Given these data, we performed several experiments to compare the two groups of English borrowings according to our annotations: comparing their frequencies, polysemy scores as well as their average similarity scores across languages. We report the obtained results in the following section.

3.2 Results

From the common vector space of the curated dataset, we obtained the cosine similarity score (between 0 and 1) for all pairs of cognates and for all pairs of languages. The distribution of these similarities is depicted in Figure 2, for each Romance language versus all other Romance languages. One notices that the distribution is unimodal, skewed to the right, with a mean similarity around 0.7. One possible explanation for the longer left tail is the inherent noise present in the relatively small dataset, which results in a bulk of less similar cognate sets.

An interesting case is the distribution of similarity between English and Romance languages cognate pairs, which seems bimodal, indicating two groups: a low similarity group, with a mean of around 0.2 similarity score, for the left curve and a high similarity one, with a mean of around 0.7 similarity score, for the right curve. In Figure 2 and Figures 3 and 4 one can observe the difference between the distribution of English versus Romance languages on the automatically generated dataset and on the curated dataset, respectively. After eliminating the errors from the dataset, the curve for the low similarity group flattened, probably because many of the eliminated errors resulted in low similarities between pairs of cognates. Still, the two distinct groups for the English cognate similarities remain visible, which demands an explanation. Our hypothesis was that the low similarity group could represent the old English borrowings from Latin, while the high similarity group could represent the recent English borrowings. To test this hypothesis, we used the manual labels for the English cognate words as old or recent borrowings and used a Mann-Whitney U Test on the two sets, to check whether the means of the two groups are actually different, shown in Table 2. It turned out that the mean differences between the two groups are not statistically significant. It might be that the bimodality is a result of noise or chance, or that there is another explanation that we have missed.

We additionally tested other hypotheses related to the difference between the two groups of English cognates, and compared the average frequency and polysemy for the two groups, which showed some statistically significant patterns. We note that the distribution of word properties such as frequency and polysemy for cognate sets have been studied before (Uban et al., 2019b, 2021) on automatically extracted cognate sets: in our study, we perform the analysis based on the curated cognate sets (providing more reliable results), as well as analyse them in relation to the two groups of English borrowings according to our annotations.

	Recent Borrw.	Old Borrw.	p-val
FR	.63	.62	.35
ES	.64	.61	.47
IT	.61	.60	.45
PT	.62	.61	.21
RO	.53	.53	.44

Table 2: Average cognate similarities for old and recent English borrowings.

In Table 3 we show the average log-frequencies

of the two groups, as well as the statistical significance of their difference. The difference in frequency is statistically significant, with very low p-values. We can see the histograms representing the frequency distributions in Figure 5. Table 4 shows the average polysemy scores for the two groups, which show a similar pattern: old borrowings have higher polysemy than recent borrowings, and so do their cognates in Romance languages. We note here that given the known dependence between frequency and polysemy (frequent words tend to be more polysemous), more experimentation is needed to confirm whether the noticed effects with regards to frequency and polysemy still manifest independently.

	Recent Borrw.	Old Borrw.	p-val
EN	3.55	4.12	4.28e-08
FR	3.52	4.06	7.33e-08
ES	3.54	4.05	2.37e-07
IT	3.59	4.10	5.04e-07
PT	3.45	3.92	3.72e-05
RO	2.33	2.93	1.36e-03

Table 3: Average (log-)frequencies for old and recent English borrowings and their cognates.

Despite the lack of a statistically significant difference between the old and the recent borrowings, we can still extract various socio-historical features that may characterize each of the two groups. Thus, the first stratum of borrowings is usually represented by concepts of primary necessity in communication, adopted through direct contact between two contemporary languages (Franco-Norman / Old French – Old English), hence become part of the fundamental lexical core of the language (e.g. *eagle, anchor, peace*, etc.). On the other hand, the more recent Latin borrowings are adopted through a cultural channel, either as lexical units circumscribed to the acrolect – often as a mere consequence of the prestige of the source language – (e.g. *celestial, diurnal, aphorism*, etc.), or as specialized terms restricted to a particular professional domain (e.g. *diameter, apostasy, atrophy*, etc.). Although most of them may be included in the category of catachrestic borrowings (according to the differentiation between catachrestic and non-catachrestic borrowings drawn by Onysko and Winter-Froemel (2011)) – as they entered the language together with the concept they designate –, the great majority of these recent Latin borrowings did not reach the shared lexicon, as a consequence of their ab-

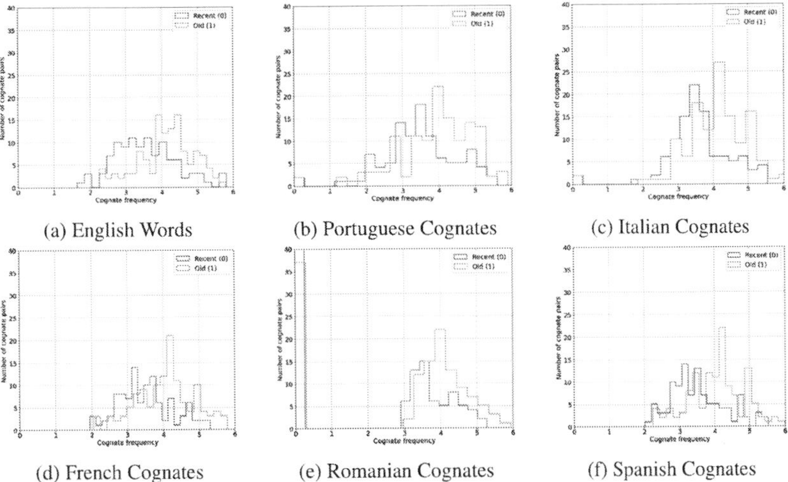

(a) English Words   (b) Portuguese Cognates   (c) Italian Cognates

(d) French Cognates   (e) Romanian Cognates   (f) Spanish Cognates

Figure 5: Distributions of (log-)frequencies for English old borrowings vs recent borrowings, and their corresponding cognates in the Romance languages.

sence in the average speaker discourse.

	Recent Borrw.	Old Borrw.	p-val
EN	3.43	5.42	6.89e-05
FR	4.38	7.04	0.002
ES	2.47	3.58	0.001
IT	2.07	3.35	7.49e-08
PT	3.16	4.00	0.02

Table 4: Average polysemy scores for old and recent English borrowings and their cognates.

4   Qualitative Analysis and Interpretation

While the initial hypothesis of an effect of the older versus more recent borrowings on semantic similarity was not supported by mean evidence, we tried to deepen our investigation by researching in detail a sample of cognate sets. We aimed to observe whether the fluctuation in the degree of similarity between the English virtual cognates, on the one hand, and their Romance correspondents, on the other hand, could be more related to the transmission channel through which they became part of the modern languages' lexica.

As we previously mentioned, the Latin borrowings in English can date from very different periods of time: some of them go back to the period of direct contact between Germanic and Latin speakers (e.g. *fork*), many of them are borrowed via Old French – thus having as a starting point in their semantic evolution the French meaning (e.g. *camp*) –, while a more recent cluster consists of loanwords taken directly from Latin (e.g. *precocious*).

We shall detail the particularities of each category by highlighting the degree of semantic similarity and by interpreting the causes of either divergence or closeness.

The example of En. *fork* is illustrative for the semantic divergence that affected the relationship between an early loanword in Celtic taken directly from Latin and its Romance virtual cognates. Lat. *furca* designated "an instrument with two arms or prongs", as well as any "Y-shaped piece of wood used as a support", including the "gallows". The distribution of meanings varied from one area of the Roman Empire to another, according to the prevalent socio-cultural domain in which a *furca* was used: the Romanian descendent of *furca* designates the instrument used in agriculture, in Spanish and Portuguese it was specialized as an instrument used for punishment, "gallows", while in English it semantically evolved to designate a refined instrument for eating. The semantic similarity between the English word and its Romance correspondents is thus very low (between 0.1 and 0.4 [French]), as the cognates reflect different semantic trajectories based on concrete socio-cultural realities.

For the second category (lexical items inherited in Old French, that were later on borrowed in English), we shall approach the case of En. *powder* "fine, dry particles produced by the grinding, crushing, or disintegration of a solid substance", borrowed from O. Fr. *poldre* "finely ground and pounded substance" (registered with this mean-

71

ing as early as the 12th century), inherited from Lat. *puluerem* "dust". Contrastingly, the other Romance languages inherited the original meaning of "dust" as their main significate (Ro. *pulbere*, It. *polvere*, Es. *polvo*, Pt. *pólvora*). That explains why the degree of similarity between English and French is higher than between English and the other Romance languages (0.75 vs 0.5). Another significant example would be that of En. *camp* "a place with temporary accommodation of huts, tents, or other structures, typically used by soldiers, refugees, or travelling people", highly divergent from its Romance virtual cognates (Ro. *câmp*, It. *campo*, Fr. *champ*, Es. *campo*, Pt. *campo*, all of them real (and true) cognates sharing the meaning of "field"). In this case, the English word is a borrowing from Fr. *camp*, in its turn borrowed from Italian, that doubled the inherited form *champ*. As it was borrowed in French as a military term – in contrast to its virtual cognates specialized in the agricultural area – it continued the same line once it penetrated the English lexicon. The degree of similarity between En. *camp* and its Romance virtual cognates is, thus, as low as 0.1 (or even lower for Portuguese).

The dataset we obtained also allows us to draw specific conclusions concerning the semantic fields where the degree of similarity is higher, regardless of the difference between real and virtual cognates, as well as of the channel through which they penetrated in English. Thus, we may observe that the terms denoting concrete or at least experimentable elements, be they animals (e.g. En. *eagle*, Ro. *acvilă*, It. *aquila*, etc.), specific materials (En. *marble*, Ro. *marmura*, It. *marmo*, etc.), or seasons (En. *autumn*, Ro. *toamnă*, etc.), show a very high degree of similarity (with the average value of 0.75), as a consequence either of their frequency (as postulated by the *law of conformity*, cf. (Hamilton et al., 2016)), either of the lack of change in the referent or in the speakers' attitude towards the referent. Equally similar from a semantic point of view are the abstract terms that designate a very particular concept which could either be circumscribed to a restricted (scientific) domain (e.g. *astronomy*, *industry*, *diameter*, *identity*, *liquid*, etc.), or did not experience any polysemic developments (thus complying with the *law of innovation*, cf. (Hamilton et al., 2016)) (e.g. *avarice*, *circumstance*, *convince*, *irony*, *presence*, etc.).

We should also draw attention to the words that were borrowed from Latin in order to cover modern concepts, absent from the source culture. It is the case of En. *consul* "an official appointed by a government to reside in a foreign country to represent the commercial interests of citizens of the appointing country", Ro. *consul*, It. *console*, etc., which show one of the highest degrees of similarity: although the word in itself existed in Classical Latin, it referred to a different political position, designating "one of the two highest magistrates at Rome".

Parallelly, it is easily understandable why words modernly created in a determined scientific domain from Latin roots have almost no semantic divergence from one language to another: once created in a contemporary language, they were naturally spread in the other languages, along with the concept newly invented. It is the case of En. *nihilism*, *optimism*, *exhaustive*, etc.

5 Conclusions

We constructed a common vector space for English and Romance languages cognate sets to analyse their similarity and thus track their semantic divergence. We analysed their similarity distribution and proposed some linguistic and historical hypotheses to explain their behaviour, especially for English cognates.

An important byproduct of our work is the curated dataset, which can be employed in other work related to semantic analysis of cognates, borrowings or false friends.

We plan to extend this study, as part of future work, to cognate similarity based on phonetic transcription and compare it to the current orthographic dataset. Moreover, we will investigate more in-depth the automatic identification of the date a word entered a language. To this end, we need to obtain a dataset that contains this information. We intend to use and adapt (Dinu, 1996) to approximate the "age" of words.

Acknowledgements

We would like to thank the reviewers for their comments. All authors contributed equally to this work. This research is supported by a grant of the Ministry of Research, Innovation and Digitization, CNCS/CCCDI – UEFISCDI, *CoToHiLi* project, project number 108, within PNCDI III.

References

Piotr Bojanowski, Edouard Grave, Armand Joulin, and Tomas Mikolov. 2016. Enriching Word Vectors with Subword Information. *arXiv preprint arXiv:1607.04606.*

Francis Bond and Kyonghee Paik. 2012. A Survey of WordNets and their Licenses. *Small*, 8(4):5.

Lyle Campbell. 1998. *Historical Linguistics. An Introduction.* MIT Press.

Santiago Castro, Jairo Bonanata, and Aiala Rosá. 2018. A High Coverage Method for Automatic False Friends Detection for Spanish and Portuguese. In *Proceedings of the Fifth Workshop on NLP for Similar Languages, Varieties and Dialects (VarDial 2018)*, pages 29–36.

Yanqing Chen and Steven Skiena. 2016. False-friend detection and entity matching via unsupervised transliteration. *arXiv preprint arXiv:1611.06722.*

Alina Maria Ciobanu and Liviu P. Dinu. 2014. Building a Dataset of Multilingual Cognates for the Romanian Lexicon. In *LREC 2014*, pages 1038–1043.

Alina Maria Ciobanu and Liviu P. Dinu. 2015. Automatic Discrimination between Cognates and Borrowings. In *Proceedings of ACL 2015, Volume 2: Short Papers*, pages 431–437.

Alina Maria Ciobanu and Liviu P. Dinu. 2019. Automatic Identification and Production of Related Words for Historical Linguistics. *Computational Linguistics*, 45(4):667–704.

Alina Maria Ciobanu and Liviu Petrisor Dinu. 2013. A Dictionary-Based Approach for Evaluating Orthographic Methods in Cognates Identification. In *Proceedings of RANLP 2013*, pages 141–147.

Alexandru Ciorănescu. 2002. *Dicţionarul etimologic al limbii române.* Saeculum, Bucharest.

Eugenio Coseriu. 1958. *Sincronía, diacronía e historia.*

Mihai Dinu. 1996. *Personalitatea Limbii Romane.* Cartea Romaneasca.

Haim Dubossarsky, Yulia Tsvetkov, Chris Dyer, and Eitan Grossman. 2015. A bottom up approach to category mapping and meaning change. In *NetWordS*, pages 66–70.

Haim Dubossarsky, Daphna Weinshall, and Eitan Grossman. 2017. Outta control: Laws of semantic change and inherent biases in word representation models. In *Proceedings of EMNLP 2017*, pages 1136–1145.

Robert Anderson Hall. 1960. *Linguistics and Your Language.* Doubleday, New York.

William L. Hamilton, Jure Leskovec, and Dan Jurafsky. 2016. Diachronic Word Embeddings Reveal Statistical Laws of Semantic Change. In *Proceedings of ACL 2016*, pages 1489–1501.

Paul Heggarty. 2012. Beyond Lexicostatistics: How to Get More out of "Word List" Comparisons. In *Quantitative Approaches to Linguistic Diversity: Commemorating the Centenary of the Birth of Morris Swadesh*, pages 113–137. Benjamins.

Diana Inkpen, Oana Frunza, and Grzegorz Kondrak. 2005. Automatic identification of cognates and false friends in french and english. In *Proceedings of RANLP 2005*, volume 9, pages 251–257.

Andrey Kutuzov, Lilja Øvrelid, Terrence Szymanski, and Erik Velldal. 2018. Diachronic word embeddings and semantic shifts: a survey. *arXiv preprint arXiv:1806.03537.*

Vladimir I. Levenshtein. 1965. Binary Codes Capable of Correcting Deletions, Insertions, and Reversals. *Soviet Physics Doklady*, 10:707–710.

April McMahon, Paul Heggarty, Robert McMahon, and Natalia Slaska. 2005. Swadesh Sublists and the Benefits of Borrowing: an Andean Case Study. *Transactions of the Philological Society*, 103(2):147–170.

Antoine Meillet. 1906. Comment les Mots Changent de Sens. In *Linguistique historique et linguistique générale*. Champion, Paris.

James W. Minett and William S.-Y. Wang. 2003. On Detecting Borrowing: Distance-based and Character-based Approaches. *Diachronica*, 20(2):289–331.

María Moliner. 2007. *Diccionario de Uso del Español.* Gredos, Madrid.

Svetlin Nakov, Preslav Nakov, and Elena Paskaleva. 2009. Unsupervised extraction of false friends from parallel bi-texts using the web as a corpus. In *Proceedings of RANLP 2009*, pages 292–298.

Charles Talbut Onions, George Washington Salisbury Friedrichsen, and Robert William Burchfield. 1994. *The Oxford Dictionary of English Etymology.* Clarendon Press, Oxford.

Alexander Onysko and Esme Winter-Froemel. 2011. Necessary loans–luxury loans? Exploring the pragmatic dimension of borrowing. *Journal of pragmatics*, 43(6):1550–1567.

Sanda Reinheimer Ripeanu. 2001. *Lingvistica Romanica: Lexic, Morfologie, Fonetica.* . BIC ALL, Bucuresti.

Sanda Reinheimer Ripeanu. 2004. *Les emprunts latins dans les langues romanes.* Editura Universităţii din Bucureşti.

Alain Rey. 2011. *Dictionnaire historique de la langue française*. Le Robert, Paris.

André Rousseau. 2000. L'évolution lexico-sémantique: explications traditionnelles et propositions nouvelles. *Théories contemporaines du changement sémantique*, pages 11–30.

Wolfgang Schweickard. 2008. Le sirene degli etimologi nel mare onomastico. le reinterpretazioni paretimologiche. *D'Achille, Paolo/Caffarelli, Enzo (edd.), Lessicografia e onomastica*, 2:83–95.

Samuel L Smith, David HP Turban, Steven Hamblin, and Nils Y Hammerla. 2017. Offline bilingual word vectors, orthogonal transformations and the inverted softmax. *arXiv preprint arXiv:1702.03859*.

Robyn Speer, Joshua Chin, Andrew Lin, Sara Jewett, and Lance Nathan. 2018. LuminosoInsight/wordfreq: v2.2.

Adam St Arnaud, David Beck, and Grzegorz Kondrak. 2017. Identifying cognate sets across dictionaries of related languages. In *Proceedings of EMNLP 2017*, pages 2519–2528.

Morris Swadesh. 1954. Perspectives and Problems of Amerindian Comparative Linguistics. *WORD*, 10(2-3):306–332.

Uri Tadmor. 2009. Loanwords in the world's languages: Findings and results. In Martin Haspelmath and Uri Tadmor, editors, *Loanwords in the World's Languages*, chapter 3, pages 55–75. De Gruyter Mouton, Berlin.

Nina Tahmasebi, Lars Borin, and Adam Jatowt. 2018. Survey of computational approaches to diachronic conceptual change. *arXiv preprint arXiv:1811.06278*.

Lianet Sepúlveda Torres and Sandra Maria Aluísio. 2011. Using machine learning methods to avoid the pitfall of cognates and false friends in Spanish-Portuguese word pairs. In *Proceedings of the 8th Brazilian Symposium in Information and Human Language Technology*.

Yulia Tsvetkov, Waleed Ammar, and Chris Dyer. 2015. Constraint-Based Models of Lexical Borrowing. In *Proceedings of NAACL-HLT 2015*, pages 598–608.

Ana Sabina Uban, Alina Ciobanu, and Liviu Dinu. 2019a. A Computational Approach to Measuring the Semantic Divergence of Cognates. In *Proceedings of CICLing 2019*. In press.

Ana Sabina Uban, Alina Ciobanu, and Liviu P Dinu. 2021. Cross-lingual Laws of Semantic Change. In Nina Tahmasebi, Lars Borin, Adam Jatowt, Yang Xu, and Simon Hengchen, editors, *Computational Approaches to Semantic Change (In press)*. Berlin: Language Science Press.

Ana Sabina Uban, Alina Maria Ciobanu, and Liviu P Dinu. 2019b. Studying Laws of Semantic Divergence across Languages using Cognate Sets. In *Proceedings of the 1st International Workshop on Computational Approaches to Historical Language Change*, pages 161–166.

Ana Sabina Uban and Liviu P Dinu. 2020. Automatically Building a Multilingual Lexicon of False Friends With No Supervision. In *Proceedings of LREC 2020*, pages 3001–3007.

Yang Xu and Charles Kemp. 2015. A Computational Evaluation of Two Laws of Semantic Change. In *CogSci*.

Author Index

Alnajjar, Khalid, 21
Arora, Aryaman, 51

Basile, Pierpaolo, 14
Basu, Samopriya, 51

Caputo, Annalina, 14
Caselli, Tommaso, 14
Cassotti, Pierluigi, 14
Chang, Ernie, 1
Cristea, Alina Maria, 64

Demberg, Vera, 1
Dinu, Anca, 64
Dinu, Liviu P., 64

Farris, Adam, 51

Georgescu, Simona, 64

Hämäläinen, Mika, 21

Kapron-King, Anna, 28
Keersmaekers, Alek, 39
Krestel, Ralf, 58
Kutuzov, Andrey, 7

Partanen, Niko, 21
Pivovarova, Lidia, 7

R, Gopalakrishnan, 51
Reke, Tim, 58
Rueter, Jack, 21

Schwanhold, Robert, 58
Shiue, Yow-Ting, 1

Uban, Ana Sabina, 64

Varvara, Rossella, 14

Xu, Yang, 28

Yeh, Hui-Syuan, 1

Zoicas, Laurentiu, 64